Reading Skills Competency Tests

THIRD LEVEL

Henriette L. Allen, Ph.D.

Henriette L. Allen, Ph.D., is a former classroom teacher in the schools of Coventry, Rhode Island, the Aramco Schools of Dhahran, Saudi Arabia, The American Community School of Benghazi, Libya, and Jackson, Mississippi. Dr. Allen served in several administrative roles, including assistant superintendent of the Jackson Public Schools. She is presently an education consultant recognized nationally. Dr. Allen is the senior author of the series *Competency Tests for Basic Reading Skills* (West Nyack, NY: The Center for Applied Research in Education). She has taught reading skills at both elementary and secondary levels, has supervised the development of a Continuous Progress Reading Program for the Jackson Public Schools, and has lectured widely in the fields of reading, classroom management, technology in the classroom, and leadership in educational administration. Dr. Allen is listed in the *World Who's Who of Women* and *Who's Who—School District Officials*. She was the 1996 recipient of the Distinguished Service Award given by the American Association of School Administrators.

Walter B. Barbe, Ph.D.

A nationally known authority in the fields of reading and learning disabilities, Walter B. Barbe, Ph.D., was for twenty-five years editor-in-chief of the widely acclaimed magazine *Highlights for Children,* and adjunct professor at The Ohio State University. Dr. Barbe is the author of over 150 professional articles and a number of books, including *Personalized Reading Instruction* (West Nyack, NY: Parker Publishing Company, Inc.), coauthored with Jerry L. Abbot. He is also the senior author and editor of two series—*Creative Growth with Handwriting* (Columbus, OH: Zaner-Bloser, Inc.) and *Barbe Reading Skills Check Lists and Activities* (West Nyack, NY: The Center for Applied Research in Education)—and he is senior editor of *Competency Tests for Basic Reading Skills*. Dr. Barbe is a fellow of the American Psychological Association and is listed in *Who's Who in America* and *American Men of Science.*

Wiley C. Thornton, M.Ed.

Wiley C. Thornton, M.Ed., is experienced in classroom teaching and educational testing and is the former research assistant in the Jackson Public Schools. His responsibilities include project evaluations, report writings, upgrading of teacher skills in interpretation and use of educational research, as well as test construction. Mr. Thornton was a frequent consultant and speaker to teacher, parent, and civic groups on educational measurement, testing, and test construction and use.

COMPETENCY TESTS FOR BASIC READING SKILLS
The Center for Applied Research in Education
West Nyack, New York 10994

Library of Congress Cataloging-in-Publication Data

Allen, Henriette L.
   Reading Skills Competency Tests : competency tests for basic
reading skills / Henriette L. Allen, Walter B. Barbe, Brandon B.
Sparkman.
        p.   cm.
   Wiley C. Thornton is named as third author on title pages of v.
2-5.
   Contents: [1] Readiness level — [2] First level — [3] Second
level — [4] Third level — [5] Fourth level — [6] Fifth level —
[7] Sixth level — [8] Advanced level.
   ISBN 0-13-021325-X (v. 1). — ISBN 0-13-021326-8 (v. 2). — ISBN
0-13-021327-6 (v. 3). — ISBN 0-13-021328-4 (v. 4). — ISBN
0-13-021329-2 (v. 5). — ISBN 0-13-021331-4 (v. 6). — ISBN
0-13-021332-2 (v. 7). — ISBN 0-13-021333-0 (v. 8).
   1. Reading Skills Competency Tests.   2. Reading—Ability testing.
I. Barbe, Walter Burke.   II. Sparkman, Brandon B.
III. Title.   IV. Title: Competency tests for basic readingskills.
LB1050.75.R43A45   1999
372.48—dc21   98-51643
                                                         CIP

© 1999 by The Center for Applied Research in Education, West Nyack, NY

Printed in the United States of America

10 9 8 7 6 5 4 3 2 1

ISBN 0-13-021328-4

ATTENTION: CORPORATIONS AND SCHOOLS

The Center for Applied Research in Education books are available at quantity discounts
with bulk purchase for educational, business, or sales promotional use. For information,
please write to: Prentice Hall Special Sales, 240 Frisch Court, Paramus, NJ 07652. Please
supply: title of book, ISBN number, quantity, how the book will be used, date needed.

THE CENTER FOR APPLIED RESEARCH
IN EDUCATION
West Nyack, NY 10994

On the World Wide Web at http://www.phdirect.com

PRENTICE-HALL INTERNATIONAL (UK) LIMITED, *LONDON*
PRENTICE-HALL OF AUSTRALIA PTY. LIMITED, *SYDNEY*
PRENTICE-HALL CANADA INC., *TORONTO*
PRENTICE-HALL HISPANOAMERICANA, S.A., *MEXICO*
PRENTICE-HALL OF INDIA PRIVATE LIMITED, *NEW DELHI*
PRENTICE-HALL OF JAPAN, INC., *TOKYO*
PEARSON EDUCATION ASIA PTE. LTD., *SINGAPORE*
EDITORA PRENTICE-HALL DO BRASIL, LTDA., *RIO DE JANEIRO*

About the *Competency Tests* for *Basic Reading Skills*

The Reading Skills Competency Tests are a practical tool designed to provide classroom teachers, reading specialists, Title I teachers and others an inventory of those reading skills mastered and those which need to be taught. The tests can be used at all levels with any reading program, as they test mastery of specific reading skills at particular levels.

For easiest use, the test materials are organized into eight distinct units tailored to evaluate children's reading skills at each of the following expectancy and difficulty levels:

Reading Skills Competency Tests: READINESS LEVEL
Reading Skills Competency Tests: FIRST LEVEL
Reading Skills Competency Tests: SECOND LEVEL
Reading Skills Competency Tests: THIRD LEVEL
Reading Skills Competency Tests: FOURTH LEVEL
Reading Skills Competency Tests: FIFTH LEVEL
Reading Skills Competency Tests: SIXTH LEVEL
Reading Skills Competency Tests: ADVANCED LEVEL

The tests give reading teachers a quick, informal means to measure the mastery of reading objectives. They can be used at any time to assess the student's competence in specific reading skills, to pinpoint specific skill weaknesses and problems, and to plan appropriate corrective or remedial instruction in an individualized reading program.

The sequence of the tests corresponds to the sequence of the well-known "Barbe Reading Skills Check Lists," which provide a complete developmental skill sequence from Readiness through Advanced Levels. Each level-unit presents ready-to-use informal tests for evaluating all skills that are listed on the Skills Check List at that level. Tests can be administered individually or to a group by a teacher or a paraprofessional.

Each unit of test materials contains:

1. Directions for using the *Reading Skills Competency Tests* at that grade level to identify individual reading needs and prescribe appropriate instruction.

2. Copies of the Skills Check List and a Group Summary Profile at that grade level for use in individual and group recordkeeping.

3. Reading Skills Competency Tests for assessing all skills at that particular grade level, including teacher test sheets with directions and answer keys for administering and evaluating each test plus reproducible student test sheets.

4. A copy of the "Barbe Reading Skills Sequential Skill Plan" chart.

For easiest use of the materials, complete directions are provided in each unit for using the Competency Tests at that level and for recording the information on the student skills Check List and the Group Summary Profile.

The test items in each level-unit correspond to the skills indicated on the Check List. The Check List can be marked to indicate which skills the child has mastered or the skills in which further instruction is needed. The Group Summary Profile can be used to obtain an overall picture of class progress and to identify the skills which need to be taught. It is also useful in identifying small groups with similar needs, students who require personalized help on a prerequisite skill, and students who need continued help on a current skill.

You will find that these tests provide for:

- quick, informal assessment of students' competence in reading skills
- diagnosis and prescription of specific reading skill weaknesses and needs
- devising of appropriate teaching strategies for individuals and small or large groups
- continuous evaluation of each child's progress in the basic reading skills
- flexibility in planning the reading instructional program
- immediate feedback to the student and the teacher

The Competency Tests for Basic Reading Skills can be used by all reading teachers in either a self-contained classroom or a team setting. They are as flexible as the teacher chooses to make them. Hopefully, they will provide an efficient, systematic means to identify the specific reading skills that students need to learn and thus meet, to a greater degree, their individual reading needs.

Henriette L. Allen

Walter B. Barbe

Contents

About the Competency Tests for Basic Reading Skills   3

How to Use the Competency Tests and Check List   9

     Begin at the Beginning   9

     Recording on the Check List   10

     Conferencing with the Pupil   10

     Conferencing with Parents   11

     Conferencing with Professional Staff   11

     Providing Check Lists to the Next Grade Level Teacher   11

     Making a Group Summary Profile from Individual Check Lists   11

     Ensuring the Sequential Presentation of Skills   11

     Using the Sequential Skill Plan Chart   12

Reading Skills Check List—Third Level   13

Group Summary Profile—Third Level   15

Reading Skills Competency Tests: Third Level   19

     I.   VOCABULARY

         A. *Recognizes 220 Dolch Basic Sight Words*   20, 22, 24, 26, 28

         B. *Word Meaning*   30

             1.   Comprehension and Use of Words   30

                 a.   Function Words   30

                 b.   Direction Words   32

                 c.   Action Words   34

                 d.   Forms of Address   36

                 e.   Career Words   38

                 f.   Color Words   40

                 g.   Metric Words   42

                 h.   Curriculum Words   44, 46

     II.   WORD ANALYSIS

         A. *Refine Phonics Skills*   48

             1.   All Initial Consonant Sounds   48, 50

             2.   Short and Long Vowel Sounds   52

             3.   Changes in Words   54

                 a.   Adding <u>s, es, d, ing, er, est</u>   54

                 b.   Dropping Final <u>e</u> and Adding <u>ing</u>   56

c. Doubling the Consonant before Adding <u>ing</u>   58

d. Changing <u>y</u> to <u>i</u> Before Adding <u>es</u>   60

4. Vowel Rules   62

    a. Vowel in One-Syllable Word Is Short   62

    b. Vowel in a Syllable or Word Ending in <u>e</u> Is Long   64

    c. Two Vowels Together, First Is Often Long and Second Is
       Silent   66

    d. Vowel Alone in Word Is Short   68

5. C Followed by <u>i, e, y</u> Makes <u>s</u> Sound   70

    C Followed by <u>a, o, u</u> Makes <u>k</u> Sound   70

6. G Followed by <u>i, e, y</u> Makes <u>j</u> Sound   72

    G Followed by <u>a, o, u</u> Makes <u>guh</u> Sound   72

7. Silent Letters in <u>kn, wr, gn</u>   74

B. *Knows Skills of:*   76

1. Forming Plurals by Adding <u>s, es, ies,</u> and by Changing <u>f</u> to <u>v</u> and
    Adding <u>es</u>   76, 78

2. Similarities of Sounds such as <u>x</u> and <u>cks</u>   80

3. Can Read Roman Numerals I, V, X   82

C. *Syllabication Rules*   84

1. There Are Usually as Many Syllables in a Word as There
    Are Vowels   84

2. When There Is a Single Consonant Between Two Vowels, the Vowel
    Goes with the First Syllable   86

3. When There Is a Double Consonant, the Syllable Break Is Between
    the Two Consonants and One Is Silent   88

D. *Can Hyphenate Words Using Syllable Rules*   90

E. *Understands Use of Primary Accent Mark*   92

F. *Knows to Accent First Syllable, Unless It Is a Prefix, Otherwise Accent
Second Syllable*   94

III. COMPREHENSION

A. *Can Find Main Idea in a Story*   96

B. *Can Keep Events in Proper Sequence*   98

C. *Can Draw Logical Conclusions*   100

D. *Is Able to See Relationships*   102

E. *Can Predict Outcomes*   104

F. *Can Follow Printed Directions*   106

G. *Can Read for a Definite Purpose* 108

  1. For Pleasure 108

  2. To Obtain Answer to Question 110

  3. To Obtain General Idea of Content 112

H. *Classify Items* 114

I. *Use Index* 116

J. *Alphabetize Words by First Two Letters* 118

K. *Knows Technique of Skimming* 120

L. *Can Determine What Source to Obtain Information* 122

M. *Use Maps and Charts* 124

IV. ORAL AND SILENT READING

A. *Oral Reading* 126

  1. Reads with Expression 126

  2. Comprehends Material Read Aloud 128

B. *Silent Reading* 132

  1. Reads Silently without Finger Pointing and Lip Movement 132

  2. Comprehends Material Read Silently 134

  3. Reads Faster Silently Than Orally 138

C. *Listening* 140

  1. Comprehends Material Read Aloud by Another 140

  2. Can Follow Directions Read Aloud 142

Barbe Reading Skills Check List Sequential Skill Plan (Chart)

How to Use the Competency Tests and Check List

A major task for teachers is verifying mastery of basic skills and keeping records. Recordkeeping and competency tests are of greater concern today than ever before. But knowing of their necessity does not make the task any easier. Competency tests and the accompanying records may be compared to a road map. One must drive through Town B to reach Town W. Competency tests are designed to assist you in verifying mastery of basic reading skills, and to indicate where to begin on the journey of reading mastery. The Reading Skills Check Lists provide check points to verify (1) where the student is on the sequence of skills, (2) when the skills were mastered, and (3) at what rate he or she is progressing.

In order for skills to develop sequentially, it is vital that we have an idea of where a student is within the sequence of reading skills. The Reading Skills Competency Tests and Check List in this unit are designed to help you teach directly to identified student needs, on a day-to-day, week-to-week, and month-to-month basis.

The Reading Skills Competency Tests are easy-to-administer tests for each reading skill on the "Barbe Reading Skills Check Lists." Directions for administering each test are given on a teacher page. This page also provides the answer key and the number of correct responses needed for mastery. Facing the teacher page is the student test page, which can be used as a master for copying when reproduction for classroom use is via copy machine.

The Check Lists are not intended as a rigid program for reading instruction. Rather they are meant to provide a general pattern around which a program may be built. The Third Level Skills Check List is divided into four major headings: Vocabulary, Word Analysis, Comprehension, and Oral and Silent Reading. Each area is of great importance to the student's development. In presenting the skills on the Check List, it is recommended that you deal alternately with some activities from each of the four major headings.

You will find a copy of the Third Level Skill Check List on page 14, which you can copy and use for individual recordkeeping.

Begin at the Beginning

Before planning an instructional program for any pupil, it is necessary to determine at what level the student is reading. This may be determined through the use of an informal reading inventory. It is then necessary to identify which basic reading skills the pupil has mastered and which skills need remediation or initial teaching.

The Competency Tests for Basic Reading Skills offer a quick, practical means to determine which skills the student has mastered and on which the student needs additional work. It is suggested that the tests be administered at the beginning of a school year. The tests may also be used at any time throughout the year to determine a student's entry point in a Reading Skills Class, or to reevaluate the progress of individual students. The tests may be given to a large group, a small group, or an individual, whichever is appropriate for those being tested and for the test being administered. Some tests, such as Oral Reading, must be administered individually. The entry point into the reading program should be at that point when a student begins to encounter difficulty with a particular reading skill.

The tests may be used as a pre test to indicate where instruction is needed, and the same tests may also be used as a post test to indicate mastery or non-mastery. Once a pupil's areas of difficulty are identified, you may then plan instructional activities accordingly. After the student has worked through a unit of instruction, you may use the same test to verify mastery of the skill. When mastery occurs, the student is advanced to another skill. When the student is unsuccessful on the specific test item, additional instruction is needed. If a reasonable amount of instruction does not result in mastery, it may be that changing instructional approaches is needed or that more work is needed on earlier skills.

Once you have decided the level of mastery tests needed, the assessing part of the reading program is ready to begin. Specific directions are given for each test. At the First Level, it is recommended that you give all directions orally. The directions for the test and what you may say to the students is on every teacher page. In some instances, as in oral reading, you may have to test each student individually.

Recording on the Check List

Recordkeeping is an important part in any instructional design. Simplicity and ease is vital. One effective method for marking a Skills Check List is as follows:

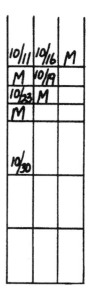

    B. Knows skills of:
      1. Forming plurals

          by adding s, es, ies

          by changing f to v and adding es

      2. Similarities of sound such as x and cks

      3. Can read Roman numerals I, V, X

    C. Syllabication rules

      1. There are usually as many syllables in a word as there are vowels

      2. Where there is a single consonant between two vowels, the vowel goes with the first syllable

      3. When there is a double consonant, the syllable break is between the two consonants and one is silent

Put an M in the first column if the pupil takes a test and demonstrates mastery of that basic reading skill. If the pupil has not mastered the skill, record the date. The date in column one indicates when instruction in the skill began. When the pupil is tested a second time, put an M in the second column if mastery is achieved, and record the date of mastery in the third column. Thus, anyone looking at the Check List can tell if the student mastered the skill before instruction or when instruction began, and when the skill was actually mastered. The Check List provides a written record of: (1) where the student is on the sequence of reading skills, (2) when the student mastered the skills, and (3) at what rate the student is progressing.

Conferencing with the Pupil

The student and teacher may discuss performance on the Competency Tests and Check List and jointly plan subsequent instruction. The Check List provides a guide for this discussion.

Conferencing with Parents

The Reading Skills Check List also serves as a guide for parent conferences. Using the Check List you can talk with parents about specific skills mastered, as well as those which have been taught but not yet fully mastered. Use of the Check List reassures parents of your concern for skill instruction, your knowledge of ways to aid their child in becoming a better reader, and of your professional plan which considers each child individually.

Conferencing with Professional Staff

Conferences with other staff such as school psychologists, counselors, and principals concerning an individual child's reading progress should focus on the instructional plan. When Check Lists are used, other professional staff members are provided with a written record of the teacher's progress and the child's progress in this program. The Check List provides information on the skills mastered, and when the skills were mastered.

Providing Check Lists to the Next Grade Level Teacher

One of the great problems in teaching reading skills at the beginning of the year is to know where to begin. If the Reading Skills Check Lists are passed along from class to class, the new teacher will know the skill level of every student in the room.

Making a Group Summary Profile from Individual Check Lists

While the Reading Skills Check List is intended primarily for individual use, there are various reasons for bringing together a record of the instructional needs of the entire class. In planning classroom strategies, you will find the use of the Group Profile on pages 16 and 17 helpful.

After you have recorded the skill level for each student on the Reading Skills Check List, you may then enter this information on the Group Profile. The Group Summary Profile is designed to help you identify groups of students who need a particular skill. It is a visual representation of the instructional needs of the entire class. It also presents the specific strengths and achievement levels of individual students.

The Group Profile may be used in conferences with supervisors and administrators to discuss the status of a particular class, the point of initial instruction, and the progress made to date. A different colored pen or pencil may be used to indicate the different grading or marking periods of the school year. This further indicates the progress the pupils have made within these periods of time.

The Group Profile can indicate the instructional materials and supplies which are needed. Since specific reading skills needs will be clearly identified, materials may be purchased which meet these needs.

Ensuring the Sequential Presentation of Skills

One of the goals of reading instruction is to develop a love of reading. But if students are to develop a love of reading, they must be able to read with efficiency. And in order to be efficient readers they must have at their ready command all of the necessary skills, including the ability to unlock new words and to read rapidly.

If the skills are to be mastered, they must be presented sequentially. When skills are presented out of sequence, critical skills are in danger of being bypassed or given minimal attention.

In many instances, the sequence of skills is firmly established; in other instances the sequence is less rigid. In these Check Lists, the skills have been placed in the order the authors feel is logical. Teachers should be free to change this sequence when there is reason to do so, being careful not to eliminate the presentation of the skill.

It is important that some skill instruction be conducted in groups. This prevents individual students from becoming isolated, a danger which sometimes occurs when too much individualization is undertaken.

Using the Sequential Skill Plan Chart

The importance of viewing the total sequential skills program cannot be minimized. The chart is intended primarily for use by the classroom teacher. If a personalized approach is used in teaching reading skills, it is still essential that the teacher view the skills as a continuous progression rather than as skills for a specific grade level. This chart allows the teacher to view not only those skills that are taught principally at the present grade placement, but also those skills which will be taught as the student progresses.

As an inservice tool, the chart provides teachers with the opportunity to see their own positions in the skills progression. It should be understood, of course, that there are any number of reasons why decisions may be made to teach the skills at levels different from those indicated on the chart. But it is important that reading skills be taught, and that basically they be taught in a sequential manner, in a planned reading program. Incidental teaching of reading skills often results in vital skills being neglected, or being bypassed until the student encounters difficulties. At that point, having to go back to earlier skills is more difficult and less effective.

The chart also provides administrators, supervisors, and teachers with direction for a total skills program.

Reading Skills Check List—
Third Level

On the following pages you will find a copy of the "Barbe Reading Skills Check List— Third Level." The Check List presents a sequential outline of the skills to be mastered at this level in four major areas: Vocabulary, Word Analysis, Comprehension, and Oral and Silent Reading.

You may photocopy the Third Level Skills Check List as many times as you need it for use in individual recordkeeping.

Accompanying the unit is a copy of the "Barbe Reading Skills Check List Sequential Skill Plan." This chart provides a visual representation of the total reading skills progression through all levels, including:

Readiness Level

First Level

Second Level

Third Level

Fourth Level

Fifth Level

Sixth Level

Advanced Level

BARBE READING SKILLS CHECK LIST
THIRD LEVEL

_____ _____ _____
(Last Name) (First Name) (Name of School)

_____ _____ _____
(Age) (Grade Placement) (Name of Teacher)

I. Vocabulary:
A. Recognizes Dolch 220 Basic Sight Words

___ a	___ done	___ I	___ out	___ these
___ about	___ don't	___ if	___ over	___ they
___ after	___ down	___ in	___ own	___ think
___ again	___ draw	___ into	___ pick	___ this
___ all	___ drink	___ is	___ play	___ those
___ always	___ eat	___ it	___ please	___ three
___ am	___ eight	___ its	___ pretty	___ to
___ an	___ every	___ jump	___ pull	___ today
___ and	___ fall	___ just	___ put	___ together
___ any	___ far	___ keep	___ ran	___ too
___ are	___ fast	___ kind	___ read	___ try
___ around	___ find	___ know	___ red	___ two
___ as	___ first	___ laugh	___ ride	___ under
___ ask	___ five	___ light	___ round	___ upon
___ ate	___ for	___ like	___ run	___ us
___ away	___ found	___ little	___ said	___ use
___ be	___ four	___ live	___ saw	___ very
___ because	___ from	___ long	___ say	___ walk
___ been	___ full	___ look	___ see	___ want
___ before	___ funny	___ made	___ seven	___ warm
___ best	___ gave	___ make	___ shall	___ was
___ better	___ get	___ many	___ she	___ wash
___ big	___ give	___ may	___ show	___ we
___ black	___ go	___ me	___ sing	___ well
___ blue	___ goes	___ much	___ sit	___ went
___ both	___ going	___ must	___ six	___ were
___ bring	___ good	___ my	___ sleep	___ what
___ brown	___ got	___ myself	___ small	___ when
___ but	___ green	___ never	___ so	___ where
___ buy	___ grow	___ new	___ some	___ which
___ by	___ had	___ no	___ soon	___ white
___ call	___ has	___ not	___ start	___ who
___ came	___ have	___ now	___ stop	___ why
___ can	___ he	___ of	___ take	___ will
___ carry	___ help	___ off	___ tell	___ wish
___ clean	___ her	___ old	___ ten	___ with
___ cold	___ here	___ on	___ thank	___ work
___ come	___ him	___ once	___ that	___ would
___ could	___ his	___ one	___ the	___ write
___ cut	___ hold	___ only	___ their	___ yellow
___ did	___ hot	___ open	___ them	___ yes
___ do	___ how	___ or	___ then	___ you
___ does	___ hurt	___ our	___ there	___ your

B. Word Meaning:
1. Comprehends and uses correctly the following words:

a. Function Words	b. Direction Words	e. Career Words	h. Curriculum Words
___ against	___ around	___ artist	___ add
___ also	___ backward	___ factory	___ American
___ being	___ forward	___ lawyer	___ country
___ during	___ left	___ mechanic	___ ecology
___ each	___ right	___ money	___ even
___ end	___ toward	___ nurse	___ fall
___ enough	**c. Action Words**	___ office	___ few
___ men	___ carry	___ operator	___ greater
___ more	___ draw	___ teacher	___ less
___ most	___ kick	___ training	___ number
___ other	___ push	___ vocation	___ odd
___ same	___ skate	**f. Color Words**	___ seasons
___ should	___ swim	___ brown	___ set
___ since	___ think	___ green	___ space
___ such	___ throw	___ orange	___ spring
___ than	___ travel	___ purple	___ state
___ though	**d. Forms of Address**	**g. Metric Words**	___ subtract
___ thought	___ Miss	___ centigrade	___ summer
___ through	___ Mr.	___ gram	___ United States
___ while	___ Mrs.	___ liter	___ winter
___ women	___ Ms.	___ meter	___ world

II. Word Analysis:
A. Refine phonics skills:
1. All initial consonant sounds
2. Short and long vowel sounds
3. Changes in words by:
   a. adding s, es, d, ed, ing, er, est
   b. dropping final e and adding ing
   c. doubling the consonant before adding ing
   d. changing y to i before adding es
4. Vowel rules
   a. vowel in one-syllable word is short
   b. vowel in syllable or word ending in e is long
   c. two vowels together, first is often long and second is silent
5. C followed by i, e, y makes s sound
   C followed by a, o, u makes k sound
6. G followed by i, e, y makes j sound
   G followed by a, o, u makes guh sound
7. Silent letters in kn, wr, gn
B. Knows skills of:
1. Forming plurals
   by adding s, es, ies
   by changing f to v and adding es
2. Similarities of sound such as x and cks (box—blocks
3. Can read Roman numerals I, V, X
C. Syllabication rules
1. There are usually as many syllables in a word as there are vowels
2. Where there is a single consonant between two vowels, the vowel goes with the first syllable (pu/pil)
3. When there is a double consonant, the syllable break is between the two consonants and one is silent (example: lit/tle)
D. Can hyphenate words using syllable rules
E. Understands use of primary accent mark
F. Knows to accent first syllable, unless it is a prefix, otherwise accent second syllable

III. Comprehension:
A. Can find main idea in story
B. Can keep events in proper sequence
C. Can draw logical conclusions
D. Is able to see relationships
E. Can predict outcomes
F. Can follow printed directions
G. Can read for a definite purpose:
1. for pleasure
2. to obtain answer to question
3. to obtain general idea of content
H. Classify items
I. Use index
J. Alphabetize words by first two letters
K. Knows technique of skimming
L. Can determine what source to obtain information (dictionary, encyclopedia, index, glossary, etc.)
M. Use maps and charts

IV. Oral and Silent Reading:
A. Oral Reading
1. Reads with expression
2. Comprehends material read aloud
B. Silent Reading
1. Reads silently without finger pointing, lip movements
2. Comprehends material read silently
3. Reads faster silently than orally
C. Listening
1. Comprehends material read aloud by another
2. Can follow directions read aloud

Group Summary Profile— Third Level

The following pages present a Group Summary Profile at the Third Level which you can use to record the progress of the entire class in mastering the specific reading skills at that level. This profile can assist you in identifying groups of students who need instruction in a particular skill as well as in assessing the strengths and achievement levels of individual students. The Group Profile may also be used in conferences with administrators to discuss the status of a particular class.

Name of Teacher: _____

GROUP SUMMARY
PROFILE
THIRD LEVEL

Student Names

	I. Vocabulary	A. Recognizes 220 Dolch Basic Sight Words	B. Word Meaning	1. Comprehends and uses correctly the following words:	Function Words	Forms of Address	Action Words	Direction Words	Metric Words	Color Words	Career Words	Curriculum Words	II. Word Analysis	A. Refine phonics skills	1. All initial consonant sounds	2. Short and long vowel sounds	3. Changes in words	4. Vowel rules	5. C sound	6. G sound	7. Silent letters in kn, wr, gn	B. Knows skills of	1. Forming plurals	2. Similarities of sound such as x and cks	3. Can read Roman numerals I, V, X	C. Syllabication rules

School: _____ Year: _____

1. There are usually as many syllables in a word as there are vowels
2. When there is a single consonant between two vowels, the vowel goes with the first syllable
3. When there is a double consonant, the syllable break is between the two consonants and one is silent
D. Can hyphenate words using syllable rules
E. Understands use of primary accent mark
F. Knows to accent first syllable, unless it is a prefix, otherwise accent second syllable
III. Comprehension
A. Can find main idea in a story
B. Can keep events in proper sequence
C. Can draw logical conclusions
D. Is able to see relationships
E. Can predict outcomes
F. Can follow printed directions
G. Can read for a definite purpose
1. for pleasure
2. to obtain answer to question
3. to obtain general idea of content
H. Classify items
I. Use index
J. Alphabetize words by first two letters
K. Knows technique of skimming
L. Can determine what source to obtain information
M. Use maps and charts
IV. Oral and Silent Reading:
A. Oral Reading
1. Reads with expression
2. Comprehends material read aloud
B. Silent Reading
1. Reads silently without finger pointing, lip movement
2. Comprehends material read silently
3. Reads faster silently than orally
C. Listening
1. Comprehends material read aloud by another
2. Can follow directions read aloud

Reading Skills Competency Tests Third Level

Henriette L. Allen, Ph.D.
Wiley C. Thornton, M.Ed.

The test items which follow are written to measure the reading skills on the "Barbe Reading Skills Check List—Third Level."

The Competency Tests and Check List provide for:

- a quick, informal assessment of a student's competence in reading skills
- diagnosis and prescription of specific reading skill weaknesses and needs
- devising of appropriate teaching strategies for individuals and small or large groups
- continuous evaluation of each student's progress in the basic reading skills
- flexibility in planning the reading instructional program
- immediate feedback to the student and the teacher

The tests are designed to give you an efficient, systematic means to identify the specific reading skills needs of students.

THIRD LEVEL

I. VOCABULARY   A. Word Recognition   1. Dolch Basic Sight Words

OBJECTIVE: The student will recognize the 220 Dolch Basic Sight Words by the end of the year.

DIRECTIONS: Part I

Option 1 Have the student say the words to the teacher or aide, noting on the student response sheet those words with which difficulty is encountered.

Option 2 Using flashcards, have the student say the words. Repeat the activity periodically until all the words have been mastered.

____	a	____	ate	____	buy
____	about	____	away	____	by
____	after	____	be	____	call
____	again	____	because	____	came
____	all	____	been	____	can
____	always	____	before	____	carry
____	am	____	best	____	clean
____	an	____	better	____	cold
____	and	____	big	____	come
____	any	____	black	____	could
____	are	____	blue	____	cut
____	around	____	both	____	did
____	as	____	bring	____	do
____	ask	____	brown	____	does
____	at	____	but		

MASTERY REQUIREMENT: Recognition of all words by the end of the school year. (See additional words on pages 22, 24, 26, and 28.)

Indicate mastery on the student response sheet with a check.

THIRD LEVEL

I. VOCABULARY

    A. Word Recognition

        1. Dolch Basic Sight Words

PART I

Name _____

Date _____

Mastery _____

_____ a	_____ ate	_____ buy
_____ about	_____ away	_____ by
_____ after	_____ be	_____ call
_____ again	_____ because	_____ came
_____ all	_____ been	_____ can
_____ always	_____ before	_____ carry
_____ am	_____ best	_____ clean
_____ an	_____ better	_____ cold
_____ and	_____ big	_____ come
_____ any	_____ black	_____ could
_____ are	_____ blue	_____ cut
_____ around	_____ both	_____ did
_____ as	_____ bring	_____ do
_____ ask	_____ brown	_____ does
_____ at	_____ but	

THIRD LEVEL

I. VOCABULARY   A. Word Recognition   1. Dolch Basic Sight Words

OBJECTIVE: The student will recognize the 220 Dolch Basic Sight Words by the end of the year.

DIRECTIONS: Part II

Option 1   Have the student say the words to the teacher or aide, noting on the student response sheet those words with which difficulty is encountered.

Option 2   Using flashcards, have the student say the words. Repeat the activity periodically until all the words have been mastered.

_____	done	_____	for	_____	grow
_____	don't	_____	found	_____	had
_____	down	_____	four	_____	has
_____	draw	_____	from	_____	have
_____	drink	_____	full	_____	he
_____	eat	_____	funny	_____	help
_____	eight	_____	gave	_____	her
_____	every	_____	get	_____	here
_____	fall	_____	give	_____	him
_____	far	_____	go	_____	his
_____	fast	_____	goes	_____	hold
_____	find	_____	going	_____	hot
_____	first	_____	good	_____	how
_____	five	_____	got	_____	hurt
_____	fly	_____	green		

MASTERY REQUIREMENT: Recognition of all words by the end of the school year. (See additional words on pages 20, 24, 26, and 28.)

Indicate mastery on the student response sheet with a check.

THIRD LEVEL

I. VOCABULARY

Name _____

   A. Word Recognition

Date _____

     1. Dolch Basic Sight Words

PART II

Mastery _____

_____	done	_____	for	_____	grow
_____	don't	_____	found	_____	had
_____	down	_____	four	_____	has
_____	draw	_____	from	_____	have
_____	drink	_____	full	_____	he
_____	eat	_____	funny	_____	help
_____	eight	_____	gave	_____	her
_____	every	_____	get	_____	here
_____	fall	_____	give	_____	him
_____	far	_____	go	_____	his
_____	fast	_____	goes	_____	hold
_____	find	_____	going	_____	hot
_____	first	_____	good	_____	how
_____	five	_____	got	_____	hurt
_____	fly	_____	green		

I. VOCABULARY   A. Word Recognition   1. Dolch Basic Sight Words

OBJECTIVE: The student will recognize the 220 Dolch Basic Sight Words by the end of the year.

DIRECTIONS: Part III

Option 1   Have the student say the words to the teacher or aide, noting on the student response sheet those words with which difficulty is encountered.

Option 2   Using flashcards, have the student say the words. Repeat the activity periodically until all the words have been mastered.

_____ I	_____ like	_____ new
_____ if	_____ little	_____ no
_____ in	_____ live	_____ not
_____ into	_____ long	_____ now
_____ is	_____ look	_____ of
_____ it	_____ made	_____ off
_____ it's	_____ make	_____ old
_____ jump	_____ many	_____ on
_____ just	_____ may	_____ once
_____ keep	_____ me	_____ one
_____ kind	_____ much	_____ only
_____ know	_____ must	_____ open
_____ laugh	_____ my	_____ or
_____ let	_____ myself	_____ our
_____ light	_____ never	

MASTERY REQUIREMENT: Recognition of all words by the end of the school year. (See additional words on pages 20, 22, 26, and 28.

Indicate mastery on the student response sheet with a check.

THIRD LEVEL

I.   VOCABULARY

    A.   Word Recognition

        1.   Dolch Basic Sight Words

Name _____

Date _____

PART III

Mastery _____

© 1999 by The Center for Applied Research in Education, Inc.

_____	I	_____	like	_____	new
_____	if	_____	little	_____	no
_____	in	_____	live	_____	not
_____	into	_____	long	_____	now
_____	is	_____	look	_____	of
_____	it	_____	made	_____	off
_____	it's	_____	make	_____	old
_____	jump	_____	many	_____	on
_____	just	_____	may	_____	once
_____	keep	_____	me	_____	one
_____	kind	_____	much	_____	only
_____	know	_____	must	_____	open
_____	laugh	_____	my	_____	or
_____	let	_____	myself	_____	our
_____	light	_____	never		

THIRD LEVEL

I. VOCABULARY A. Word Recognition 1. Dolch Basic Sight Words

OBJECTIVE: The student will recognize the 220 Dolch Basic Sight Words by the end of the year.

DIRECTIONS: Part IV

Option 1 Have the student say the words to the teacher or aide, noting on the student response sheet those words with which difficulty is encountered.

Option 2 Using flashcards, have the student say the words. Repeat the activity periodically until all the words have been mastered.

_____ out	_____ run	_____ some
_____ over	_____ said	_____ soon
_____ own	_____ saw	_____ start
_____ pick	_____ say	_____ stop
_____ play	_____ see	_____ take
_____ please	_____ seven	_____ tell
_____ pretty	_____ shall	_____ ten
_____ pull	_____ she	_____ thank
_____ put	_____ show	_____ that
_____ ran	_____ sing	_____ the
_____ read	_____ sit	_____ their
_____ red	_____ six	_____ them
_____ ride	_____ sleep	_____ then
_____ right	_____ small	_____ there
_____ round	_____ so	

MASTERY REQUIREMENT: Recognition of all words by the end of the school year. (See additional words on pages 20, 22, 24, and 28.)

Indicate mastery on the student response sheet with a check.

THIRD LEVEL

I. **VOCABULARY**

    A. **Word Recognition**

        1. **Dolch Basic Sight Words**

PART IV

Name _____

Date _____

Mastery _____

_____	out	_____	run	_____	some
_____	over	_____	said	_____	soon
_____	own	_____	saw	_____	start
_____	pick	_____	say	_____	stop
_____	play	_____	see	_____	take
_____	please	_____	seven	_____	tell
_____	pretty	_____	shall	_____	ten
_____	pull	_____	she	_____	thank
_____	put	_____	show	_____	that
_____	ran	_____	sing	_____	the
_____	read	_____	sit	_____	their
_____	red	_____	six	_____	them
_____	ride	_____	sleep	_____	then
_____	right	_____	small	_____	there
_____	round	_____	so		

I. VOCABULARY   A. Word Recognition   1. Dolch Basic Sight Words

OBJECTIVE: The student will recognize the 220 Dolch Basic Sight Words by the end of the year.

DIRECTIONS: Part V

Option 1   Have the student say the words to the teacher or aide, noting on the student response sheet those words with which difficulty is encountered.

Option 2   Using flashcards, have the student say the words. Repeat the activity periodically until all the words have been mastered.

_____	these	_____	us	_____	which
_____	they	_____	use	_____	white
_____	think	_____	very	_____	who
_____	this	_____	walk	_____	why
_____	those	_____	want	_____	will
_____	three	_____	warm	_____	wish
_____	to	_____	was	_____	with
_____	today	_____	wash	_____	work
_____	together	_____	we	_____	would
_____	too	_____	well	_____	write
_____	try	_____	went	_____	yellow
_____	two	_____	were	_____	yes
_____	under	_____	what	_____	you
_____	up	_____	when	_____	your
_____	upon	_____	where		

MASTERY REQUIREMENT: Recognition of all words by the end of the school year. (See additional words on pages 20, 22, 24, and 26.)

Indicate mastery on the student response sheet with a check.

THIRD LEVEL

I. VOCABULARY

Name _____

   A. Word Recognition

Date _____

     1. Dolch Basic Sight Words

PART V

Mastery _____

_____ these	_____ us	_____ which
_____ they	_____ use	_____ white
_____ think	_____ very	_____ who
_____ this	_____ walk	_____ why
_____ those	_____ want	_____ will
_____ three	_____ warm	_____ wish
_____ to	_____ was	_____ with
_____ today	_____ wash	_____ work
_____ together	_____ we	_____ would
_____ too	_____ well	_____ write
_____ try	_____ went	_____ yellow
_____ two	_____ were	_____ yes
_____ under	_____ what	_____ you
_____ up	_____ when	_____ your
_____ upon	_____ where	

I. VOCABULARY   B. Word Meaning   1. Comprehension and use of words

a. Function words

OBJECTIVE: The student will be able to comprehend and use "function" words.

DIRECTIONS: From the list of words above each of the following sentences, select the word that will best fill the blank in each sentence.

| also | each | most | since |

1. On our trip, Mother did some of the driving, but Dad drove ___most___ of the way.
2. Jenny has not had a sore throat ___since___ she had her tonsils out.
3. If Alice and Richard go, Doris may go ___also___ .
4. There was one present for ___each___ person in the family.

| against | end | same | while |

5. We cleared the middle of the room by pushing our desks back ___against___ the wall.
6. Although both of their birthdays are August 5, they were not born the ___same___ year.
7. Mother waited in the car ___while___ I went to buy the tickets.
8. If he misses a turn, he will have to go to the ___end___ of the line.

| during | more | other | should | thought |

9. There are times that we ___should___ do things that we do not want to do.
10. Jan's team won ___more___ games than anyone else.
11. I did better on that science test than I ___thought___ I would.
12. Did it rain ___during___ the night?
13. Peggy is Don's ___other___ sister.

| enough | men | through | women |

14. Do you have ___enough___ money for a drink and a sandwich?
15. Boys grow up to be ___men___ .
16. Girls grow up to be ___women___ .
17. Are you ___through___ reading that book?

| being | such | than | though |

18. Jimmy is oldest, so he had more work to do ___than___ anyone else.
19. Seeing the game on TV is fun, but not as good as really ___being___ there.
20. Mother will try to go, ___though___ she does not have much time.
21. Is there ___such___ a word as "sporky?"

MASTERY REQUIREMENT: 17 correct responses

Indicate mastery on the student response sheet with a check.

THIRD LEVEL

I. VOCABULARY

Name _____

B. Word Meaning

Date _____

1. Comprehension and use of words

a. Function words

Mastery _____

DIRECTIONS: From the list of words above each of the following groups of sentences, select the word that will best fill the blank in each sentence.

also   each   most   since

1. On our trip, Mother did some of the driving, but Dad drove _____ of the way.
2. Jenny has not had a sore throat _____ she had her tonsils out.
3. If Alice and Richard go, Doris may go _____ .
4. There was one present for _____ person in the family.

against   end   same   while

5. We cleared the middle of the room by pushing our desks back _____ the wall.
6. Although both of their birthdays are August 5, they were not born the _____ year.
7. Mother waited in the car _____ I went to buy the tickets.
8. If he misses a turn, he will have to go to the _____ of the line.

during   more   other   should   thought

9. There are times that we _____ do things that we do not want to do.
10. Jan's team won _____ games than anyone else.
11. I did better on that science test than I _____ I would.
12. Did it rain _____ the night?
13. Peggy is Don's _____ sister.

enough   men   through   women

14. Do you have _____ money for a drink and a sandwich?
15. Boys grow up to be _____ .
16. Girls grow up to be _____ .
17. Are you _____ reading that book?

being   such   than   though

18. Jimmy is oldest, so he had more work to do _____ anyone else.
19. Seeing the game on TV is fun, but not as good as really _____ there.
20. Mother will try to go, _____ she does not have much time.
21. Is there _____ a word as "sporky?"

THIRD LEVEL

I. VOCABULARY   B. Word Meaning   1. Comprehension and use of words

b. Direction words

OBJECTIVE: The student will be able to comprehend and use "direction" words.

DIRECTIONS: From the list of words above each of the following groups of sentences, select the word that will best fill the blank in each sentence.

around   left   toward

1. Susan is helping her father build a fence ____around____ their garden.

2. Johnny tripped as he ran ____toward____ the goal line.

3. Move the post just a bit to the ____left____ and it will be in line.

backward   forward   right

4. On a map, east is to the . ____right____ .

5. To move ahead means to go ____forward____ .

6. There was no room for Dick to turn around in the tunnel, so he had to crawl out ____backward____ .

MASTERY REQUIREMENT: All correct

Indicate mastery on the student response sheet with a check.

I. VOCABULARY

Name _____

B. Word Meaning

Date _____

1. Comprehension and use
of words

Mastery _____

b. Direction words

DIRECTIONS: From the list of words above each of the following groups
of sentences, select the word that will best fill the blank in
each sentence.

around   left   toward

1. Susan is helping her father build a fence _____ their
garden.

2. Johnny tripped as he ran _____ the goal line.

3. Move the post just a bit to the _____ and it will be in
line.

backward   forward   right

4. On a map, east is to the _____.

5. To move ahead means to go _____.

6. There was no room for Dick to turn around in the tunnel, so he had to

crawl out _____.

THIRD LEVEL

I.   VOCABULARY   B.   Word Meaning   1.   Comprehension and use of words

c.   Action words

OBJECTIVE: The student will be able to comprehend and use "action" words.

DIRECTIONS: From the list of words above each of the following groups of sentences, select the word that will best fill the blank in each sentence.

carry   kick   skate   think

1.   Please be quiet while I ___think___ about this math problem.

2.   Help me ___carry___ this post out to the barn.

3.   If you get behind that spotted pony, he will ___kick___ you.

4.   Which is the easiest way to ___skate___, roller or ice?

draw   push   swim   throw   travel

5.   Can you ___swim___ the length of the pool?

6.   How far can you ___throw___ a softball?

7.   During the summer we are planning to ___travel___ to several places we have never been before.

8.   I would like to ___draw___ a picture of that old house and barn.

9.   We ran out of gas and had to ___push___ the car to the side of the road.

MASTERY REQUIREMENT: All correct

Indicate mastery on the student response sheet with a check.

I. VOCABULARY

  B. Word Meaning

    1. Comprehension and use
        of words

      c. Action words

DIRECTIONS: From the list of words above each of the following groups
             of sentences, select the word which will best fill the blank
             in each sentence.

        carry   kick   skate   think

1. Please be quiet while I _____ about this math problem.

2. Help me _____ this post out to the barn.

3. If you get behind that spotted pony, he will _____ you.

4. Which is the easiest way to _____, roller or ice?

        draw   push   swim   throw   travel

5. Can you _____ the length of the pool?

6. How far can you _____ a softball?

7. During the summer we are planning to _____ to several
    places we have never been before.

8. I would like to _____ a picture of that old house and
    barn.

9. We ran out of gas and had to _____ the car to the side of
    the road.

THIRD LEVEL

I. VOCABULARY   B. Word Meaning   1. Comprehension and use of words

d. Forms of address

OBJECTIVE: The student will be able to comprehend and use forms of address.

PART I:

DIRECTIONS: Match the following by writing the proper letter in the blank.

_c_	1.	Miss	a.	Form of address for a man
_a_	2.	Mr.	b.	Form of address for a married lady
_b_	3.	Mrs.	c.	Form of address for an unmarried lady
_d_	4.	Ms.	d.	Form of address which may be used for a married or unmarried lady

PART II:

DIRECTIONS: Write the correct form of address on the blank line for each of the following.

1.   __Mr.__   Smith is a baker. He is my friend.

2.   __Miss__   Jones is planning to get married. She has already set the date.

3.   When she gets married, her title will change from Miss to __Mrs.__ .

4.   My neighbor, __Mr.__   John Lewis, has just won the election.

5.   When in doubt whether a lady is married or unmarried, one should use the title __Ms.__ .

6.   My teacher's title is _____.

MASTERY REQUIREMENT: 8 correct responses

Indicate mastery on the student response sheet with a check.

I. VOCABULARY

   B. Word Meaning

      1. Comprehension and use
         of words

         d. Forms of address

PART I:

DIRECTIONS: Match the following by writing the proper letter in the blank.

_____ 1. Miss   a.   Form of address for a man

_____ 2. Mr.   b.   Form of address for a married lady

_____ 3. Mrs.   c.   Form of address for an unmarried lady

_____ 4. Ms.   d.   Form of address which may be used for a married or unmarried lady

PART II:

DIRECTIONS: Write the correct form of address on the blank line for each of the following.

1. _____ Smith is a baker. He is my friend.

2. _____ Jones is planning to get married. She has already set the date.

3. When she gets married, her title will change from Miss to _____.

4. My neighbor, _____ John Lewis, has just won the election.

5. When in doubt whether a lady is married or unmarried, one should use the title _____.

6. My teacher's title is _____.

THIRD LEVEL

I. VOCABULARY   B. Word Meaning   1. Comprehension and use of words

e. Career words

OBJECTIVE: The student will comprehend and use "career" words correctly.

PART I:

DIRECTIONS: Match the words in Column 1 with the right meanings in Column 2.

Column 1		Column 2	
c	1. artist	a.	A place where manufacturing is done
a	2. factory	b.	Can be exchanged for things which are wanted or needed
b	3. money		
e	4. teacher	c.	One who produces objects of beauty
d	5. training	d.	The preparing of someone for work of a certain kind
		e.	One who instructs

PART II:

DIRECTIONS: Match the words in Column 1 with the right meanings in Column 2.

Column 1		Column 2	
e	1. lawyer	a.	One who works with doctors or in hospitals to help sick people
d	2. mechanic	b.	A person's work or job
a	3. nurse	c.	A place where business is done
c	4. office	d.	One who repairs things
f	5. operator	e.	One who helps people with legal problems
b	6. vocation	f.	One who causes an object or tool to perform work

MASTERY REQUIREMENT: 9 correct responses

Indicate mastery on the student response sheet with a check.

THIRD LEVEL

I. VOCABULARY

Name _____

B. Word Meaning

Date _____

   1. Comprehension and use of words

Mastery _____

      e. Career words

PART I:

DIRECTIONS: Match the words in Column 1 with the right meanings in Column 2.

Column 1		Column 2
_____ 1.	artist	a. A place where manufacturing is done
_____ 2.	factory	b. Can be exchanged for things which are wanted or needed
_____ 3.	money	c. One who produces objects of beauty
_____ 4.	teacher	d. The preparing of someone for work of a certain kind
_____ 5.	training	e. One who instructs

PART II:

DIRECTIONS: Match the words in Column 1 with the right meanings in Column 2.

Column 1		Column 2
_____ 1.	lawyer	a. One who works with doctors or in hospitals to help sick people
_____ 2.	mechanic	b. A person's work or job
_____ 3.	nurse	c. A place where business is done
_____ 4.	office	d. One who repairs things
_____ 5.	operator	e. One who helps people with legal problems
_____ 6.	vocation	f. One who causes an object or tool to perform work

I.   VOCABULARY   B.   Word Meaning   1.   Comprehension and use of words

f.   Color words

OBJECTIVE: The student will comprehend and use "color" words correctly.

DIRECTIONS: Select one of the words from the following list to fill the blank in each of the sentences.

brown   green   orange   purple

1. Tame rabbits are often white or gray, but wild rabbits are nearly always ___brown___ .

2. We could tell he was the king because he was wearing a ___purple___ robe.

3. A citrus fruit whose name is the same as its color is the ___orange___ .

4. During the summer, the leaves and grass are ___green___ .

5. Most fur coats are the color ___brown___ .

6. ___Orange___ pumpkins grew in the farmer's garden.

7. On Saint Patrick's Day many people wear the color ___green___ .

8. When the grass dies in the fall, it turns ___brown___ .

9. The color word that is divided into syllables between two consonants is ___purple___ .

10. The Christmas colors are red and ___green___ .

MASTERY REQUIREMENT: 8 correct responses

Indicate mastery on the student response sheet with a check.

I. VOCABULARY

Name _____

B. Word Meaning

Date _____.

1. Comprehension and use of words

f. Color words

Mastery _____

DIRECTIONS: Select one of the words from the following list to fill the blank in each of the sentences.

brown   green   orange   purple

1. Tame rabbits are often white or gray, but wild rabbits are nearly always

_____.

2. We could tell he was the king because he was wearing a _____ robe.

3. A citrus fruit whose name is the same as its color is the _____.

4. During the summer, the leaves and grass are _____.

5. Most fur coats are the color _____.

6. _____ pumpkins grew in the farmer's garden.

7. On Saint Patrick's Day many people wear the color _____.

8. When the grass dies in the fall, it turns _____.

9. The color word that is divided into syllables between two consonants is _____.

10. The Christmas colors are red and _____.

THIRD LEVEL

I. VOCABULARY   B. Word Meaning   1. Comprehension and use of words

g. Metric words

OBJECTIVE: The students will comprehend and use "metric" words correctly.

PART I:

DIRECTIONS: Match the following by writing the correct letter in the blank.

_c_	1.	Centigrade	a.	Metric measure of weight
_a_	2.	Gram	b.	Metric measure of length
_d_	3.	Liter	c.	A measure of temperature
_b_	4.	Meter	d.	Metric measure of volume

PART II:

DIRECTIONS: Fill in the correct metric word for each of the following sentences.

centigrade   gram   liter   meter

1. Today it is 25° _____centigrade_____.

2. A _____meter_____ of ribbon is longer than a yard of ribbon.

3. Some radio stations give both Fahrenheit and _____centigrade_____ temperature readings.

4. In England, milk is sold by the _____liter_____.

5. Miles are measured by _____meters_____.

6. Meat is weighed by the _____gram_____ in most countries.

MASTERY REQUIREMENT: 8 correct responses

Indicate mastery on the student response sheet with a check.

THIRD LEVEL

I. VOCABULARY

Name _____

   B. Word Meaning

Date _____

      1. Comprehension and use
          of words

Mastery _____

         g. Metric words

PART I:

DIRECTIONS: Match the following by writing the correct letter in the blank.

_____ 1. Centigrade   a. Metric measure of weight

_____ 2. Gram   b. Metric measure of length

_____ 3. Liter   c. A measure of temperature

_____ 4. Meter   d. Metric measure of volume

PART II:

DIRECTIONS: Fill in the correct metric word for each of the following sentences.

centigrade   gram   liter   meter

1. Today it is 25° _____.

2. A _____ of ribbon is longer than a yard of ribbon.

3. Some radio stations give both Fahrenheit and _____ temperature readings.

4. In England, milk is sold by the _____.

5. Miles are measured by _____.

6. Meat is weighed by the _____ in most countries.

THIRD LEVEL

I.   VOCABULARY   B.   Word Meaning   1.   Comprehension and use of words

h.   Curriculum words

OBJECTIVE: The student will comprehend and use "curriculum" words correctly.

DIRECTIONS: Match the definition with the word by writing the correct letter on the blank line to the left.

_d_	1.	add	a.	A group of similar things
_j_	2.	ecology	b.	Not many
_f_	3.	even	c.	Not as many
_b_	4.	few	d.	Obtain a sum
_k_	5.	greater	e.	An emptiness or open place
_c_	6.	less	f.	Can be grouped by two
_i_	7.	number	g.	Cannot be grouped by two
_g_	8.	odd	h.	Obtain a difference
_a_	9.	set	i.	A unit we count by
_e_	10.	space	j.	The study of the way man and nature live together
_h_	11.	subtract	k.	More than or larger than

MASTERY REQUIREMENT: 9 correct responses (See additional words on page 46.)

Indicate mastery on student response sheet with a check.

THIRD LEVEL

I. VOCABULARY

B. Word Meaning

1. Comprehension and use
of words

h. Curriculum words

Name _____

Date _____

Mastery _____

DIRECTIONS: Match the definition with the word by writing the correct
letter on the blank line to the left.

_____ 1. add   a. A group of similar things

_____ 2. ecology   b. Not many

_____ 3. even   c. Not as many

_____ 4. few   d. Obtain a sum

_____ 5. greater   e. An emptiness or open place

_____ 6. less   f. Can be grouped by two

_____ 7. number   g. Cannot be grouped by two

_____ 8. odd   h. Obtain a difference

_____ 9. set   i. A unit we count by

_____ 10. space   j. The study of the way man and nature
                              live together

_____ 11. subtract   k. More than or larger than

THIRD LEVEL

I. **VOCABULARY**   B. Word Meaning   1. Comprehension and use of words

                                 h. Curriculum words

OBJECTIVE: The student will comprehend and use "curriculum" words correctly.

DIRECTIONS: Match the definition with the word by writing the correct letter on the blank line next to each word.

_g_	1.	American	a.	The four parts of the year
_c_	2.	country	b.	The earth and everything on it
_d_	3.	fall	c.	A section of land and population of people under one government
_a_	4.	seasons		
_j_	5.	spring	d.	Also known as autumn
_f_	6.	state	e.	The country we live in
_i_	7.	summer	f.	One of the fifty parts of our country
_e_	8.	United States	g.	A person who lives in our country
_h_	9.	winter	h.	The coldest part of the year
_b_	10.	world	i.	The hottest part of the year
			j.	Between winter and summer

MASTERY REQUIREMENT: 9 correct responses (See additional words on page 44.)

Indicate mastery on the student response sheet with a check.

THIRD LEVEL

I. VOCABULARY

   B. Word Meaning

      1. Comprehension and use
         of words

        h. Curriculum words

Name _____

Date _____

Mastery _____

DIRECTIONS: Match the definition with the word by writing the correct letter on the blank line next to each word.

_____ 1. American

_____ 2. country

_____ 3. fall

_____ 4. seasons

_____ 5. spring

_____ 6. state

_____ 7. summer

_____ 8. United States

_____ 9. winter

_____ 10. world

a. The four parts of the year

b. The earth and everything on it

c. A section of land and population of people under one government

d. Also known as autumn

e. The country we live in

f. One of the fifty parts of our country

g. A person who lives in our country

h. The coldest part of the year

i. The hottest part of the year

j. Between winter and summer

II. WORD ANALYSIS   A.   Refine Phonics Skills   1.   Initial consonant sounds

OBJECTIVE: The student will know all initial consonant sounds.

DIRECTIONS: Below are two groups of words. In each group, match each word with its beginning sound.

GROUP ONE

1.	does	8	z
2.	fire	3	s
3.	some	5	j
4.	well	1	d
5.	just	4	w
6.	ring	2	f
7.	tiny	7	t
8.	zero	9	n
9.	never	6	r

GROUP TWO

1.	best	4	l
2.	here	9	y
3.	kind	2	h
4.	like	6	p
5.	mean	1	b
6.	penny	5	m
7.	quiet	8	v
8.	very	7	q
9.	yellow	3	k

MASTERY REQUIREMENT: 15 correct responses (See additional sounds on page 50.)

Indicate mastery on the student response sheet with a check.

II. WORD ANALYSIS

    A. Refine Phonics Skills

        1. Initial consonant sounds

Name _____

Date _____

Mastery _____

DIRECTIONS: Below are two groups of words. In each group, match each word with its beginning sound.

GROUP ONE

1. does   _____ z
2. fire   _____ s
3. some   _____ j
4. well   _____ d
5. just   _____ w
6. ring   _____ f
7. tiny   _____ t
8. zero   _____ n
9. never   _____ r

GROUP TWO

1. best   _____ l
2. here   _____ y
3. kind   _____ h
4. like   _____ p
5. mean   _____ b
6. penny   _____ m
7. quiet   _____ v
8. very   _____ q
9. yellow   _____ k

THIRD LEVEL

II.   WORD ACTIVITIES   A.   Refine Phonics Skills   1.   Initial consonant sounds

OBJECTIVE: The student will know all initial consonant sounds.

DIRECTIONS: Below are three groups of words. In each group, match each word with its beginning sound.

GROUP ONE

1.	bring	9	bl
2.	cream	5	th
3.	swing	2	cr
4.	shine	4	sh
5.	third	8	wh
6.	chair	11	cl
7.	smile	1	br
8.	white	10	gl
9.	blue	7	sm
10.	glass	6	ch
11.	close	3	sw

GROUP TWO

1.	please	6	sn
2.	green	10	fl
3.	scare	8	dr
4.	from	5	pr
5.	pretty	9	st
6.	snail	2	gr
7.	travel	3	sc
8.	drain	1	pl
9.	stamp	7	tr
10.	flower	4	fr

GROUP THREE

1.	scream	3	chr
2.	string	6	thr
3.	Christmas	1	scr
4.	school	4	sch
5.	spring	2	str
6.	throw	5	spr

MASTERY REQUIREMENT: 23 correct responses (See additional sounds on page 48.)

Indicate mastery on the student response sheet with a check.

II. **WORD ANALYSIS**

Name _____

A. Refine Phonics Skills

1. Initial consonant sounds

Date _____

Mastery _____

DIRECTIONS: Below are three groups of words. In each group, match each word with its beginning sound.

GROUP ONE

1. bring   _____ bl
2. cream   _____ th
3. swing   _____ cr
4. shine   _____ sh
5. third   _____ wh
6. chair   _____ cl
7. smile   _____ br
8. white   _____ gl
9. blue   _____ sm
10. glass   _____ ch
11. close   _____ sw

GROUP TWO

1. please   _____ sn
2. green   _____ fl
3. scare   _____ dr
4. from   _____ pr
5. pretty   _____ st
6. snail   _____ gr
7. travel   _____ sc
8. drain   _____ pl
9. stamp   _____ tr
10. flower   _____ fr

GROUP THREE

1. scream   _____ chr
2. string   _____ thr
3. Christmas _____ scr
4. school   _____ sch
5. spring   _____ str
6. throw   _____ spr

II. WORD ANALYSIS   A.   Refine Phonics Skills   2.   Short and long vowel sounds

OBJECTIVE: The student will distinguish long and short vowel sounds.

DIRECTIONS: Say each word silently. If the vowel *that you hear* is long, write the word in the column under LONG; if it is short, write the word in the column under SHORT.

	LONG	SHORT
1. tan	_____	___tan___
2. same	___same___	_____
3. please	___please___	_____
4. shed	_____	___shed___
5. spite	___spite___	_____
6. flit	_____	___flit___
7. dog	_____	___dog___
8. bloat	___bloat___	_____
9. gull	_____	___gull___
10. cue	___cue___	_____

MASTERY REQUIREMENT: 9 correct responses

Indicate mastery on the student response sheet with a check.

II. WORD ANALYSIS

Name _____

   A. Refine Phonics Skills

Date _____ _____

      2. Short and long vowel
          sounds

Mastery _____

DIRECTIONS: Say each word silently. If the vowel *that you hear* is long, write the word in the column under LONG; if it is short, write the word in the column under SHORT.

	LONG	SHORT
1. tan	_____	_____
2. same	_____	_____
3. please	_____	_____
4. shed	_____	_____
5. spite	_____	_____
6. flit	_____	_____
7. dog	_____	_____
8. bloat	_____	_____
9. gull	_____	_____
10. cue	_____	_____

II. WORD ANALYSIS   A.   Refine Phonics Skills   3.   Changes in words

a.   Adding s, es, d , ed, ing, er, est

OBJECTIVE: The student will change words by adding the proper ending, choosing from s, es, d, ed, ing, er, est.

DIRECTIONS: Fill the blanks in these sentences by placing the proper ending on the word at the end of the sentence. Choose from this list of endings:

s   es   d   ed   ing   er   est

1. How many ____days____ will it be before we have a holiday?   day _____

2. Pete is ____older____ than his sister.   old _____

3. Jan ____goes____ to California every summer.   go _____

4. Sarah is the ___smartest___ girl in the class.   smart _____

5. When will you be through ___building___ that thing?   build _____

6. How long have you ____owed____ me that dime?   owe _____

7. We ____talked____ for a long time yesterday.   talk _____

8. Two ____boxes____ fell off the back of the truck.   box _____

9. Frank is ____working____ in a grocery store on Saturdays.   work _____

10. It has ____rained____ only two times this month.   rain _____

11. She is the ____fastest____ swimmer on the team.   fast _____

12. The tug ____whistled___ as it chugged up the river.   whistle _____

MASTERY REQUIREMENT: 9 correct responses

Indicate mastery on the student response sheet with a check.

II. WORD ANALYSIS   Name _____

   A. Refine Phonics Skills

      3. Changes in words   Date _____

         a. Adding e, es, d, ed,   Mastery_____
            ing, er, est

DIRECTIONS: Fill the blanks in these sentences by placing the proper ending on the word at the end of the sentence. Choose from this list of endings:

s   es   d   ed   ing   er   est

1. How many _____ will it be before we have a holiday?   day _____

2. Pete is _____ than his sister.   old _____

3. Jan _____ to California every summer.   go _____

4. Sarah is the _____ girl in the class.   smart _____

5. When will you be through _____ that thing?   build _____

6. How long have you _____ me that dime?   owe _____

7. We _____ for a long time yesterday.   talk _____

8. Two _____ fell off the back of the truck.   box _____

9. Frank is _____ in a grocery store on Saturdays.   work _____

10. It has _____ only two times this month.   rain _____

11. She is the _____ swimmer on the team.   fast _____

12. The tug _____ as it chugged up the river.   whistle _____

II.   WORD ANALYSIS   A.   Refine Phonics Skills   3.   Changes in words

                                                     b.   Dropping e and adding ing

OBJECTIVE: The student will correctly drop the final e in words before adding ing.

DIRECTIONS: Fill the blank in each sentence by using the correct form of the word at the end of the sentence.

1.   The sun is ____shining____ brightly.   ____shine____

2.   Are you ____writing____ a letter to your uncle?   ____write____

3.   May I borrow your hatchet when you are through ____using____ it?   ____use____

4.   She fell down the steps as we were ____leaving____ .   ____leave____

5.   Jack has been ____saving____ money for Christmas all year.   ____save____

6.   Look at the cattle ____grazing____ in the pasture.   ____graze____

7.   How long has Beth been ____serving____ as president?   ____serve____

8.   The cars were ____sliding____ on the icy roads.   ____slide____

9.   What are you ____giving____ John for his birthday?   ____give____

10. Ann is ____making____ a new toy for her brother.   ____make____

MASTERY REQUIREMENT: 8 correct responses

Indicate mastery on the student response sheet with a check.

56

II. WORD ANALYSIS   Name _____

    A. Refine Phonics Skills
                               Date_____

        3. Changes in words

           b. Dropping e and adding ing   Mastery _____

DIRECTIONS: Fill the blank in each sentence by using the correct form
                     of the word at the end of the sentence.

1. The sun is _____ brightly.   shine

2. Are you _____ a letter to your uncle?   write

3. May I borrow your hatchet when you are through

    _____ it?   use

4. She fell down the steps as we were _____.   leave

5. Jack has been _____ money for Christmas   save
    all year.

6. Look at the cattle _____ in the pasture.   graze

7. How long has Beth been _____ as president?   serve

8. The cars were _____ on the icy roads.   slide

9. What are you _____ John for his birthday?   give

10. Ann is _____ a new toy for her brother.   make

II. WORD ANALYSIS   A. Refine Phonics Skills   3. Changes in words

c. Doubling consonant before adding <u>ing</u>

OBJECTIVE: The student will correctly double the final consonant in words before adding <u>ing</u>.

DIRECTIONS: Fill the blank in each sentence by using the correct form of the word at the end of the sentence.

1. The ___swimming___ pool opens at noon on Sunday.   ___swim___

2. Mother is outside ___digging___ in her flower bed.   ___dig___

3. Have you been ___sitting___ there long?   ___sit___

4. Stop ___grabbing___ my arm!   ___grab___

5. He missed three spelling words for not ___dotting___ an "i."   ___dot___

6. Sue was the ___batting___ champion of her softball league.   ___bat___

7. Two deer came ___running___ across the field.   ___run___

8. A policeman was ___stopping___ all trucks on the highway.   ___stop___

9. The doorbell rang while I was ___putting___ on my coat.   ___put___

10. I am ___shutting___ the gate to keep rabbits out of the garden.   ___shut___

MASTERY REQUIREMENT: 9 correct responses

Indicate mastery on the student response sheet with a check.

II. WORD ANALYSIS   Name _____

   A. Refine Phonics Skills

      Date _____

    3. Changes in words

       c. Doubling consonant   Mastery _____
          before adding <u>ing</u>

DIRECTIONS: Fill the blank in each sentence by using the correct form of the word at the end of the sentence.

1. The _____ pool opens at noon on Sunday.   _____swim_____

2. Mother is outside _____ in her flower bed.   _____dig_____

3. Have you been _____ there long?   _____sit_____

4. Stop _____ my arm!   _____grab_____

5. He missed three spelling words for not
    _____ an "i."   _____dot_____

6. Sue was the _____ champion of her
    softball league.   _____bat_____

7. Two deer came _____ across the field.   _____run_____

8. A policeman was _____ all trucks on the
    highway.   _____stop_____

9. The doorbell rang while I was _____ on
    my coat.   _____put_____

10. I am _____ the gate to keep rabbits out
     of the garden.   _____shut_____

THIRD LEVEL

II. WORD ANALYSIS   A.   Refine Phonics Skills   3.   Changes in words

                                                d.   Changing y to i before adding es

OBJECTIVE: The student will correctly change y to i before adding es.

DIRECTIONS: Fill the blank in each sentence by using the correct form of the word at the end of the sentence.

1. My kite _____flies_____ better than yours does.   __fly__

2. How many _____tries_____ do you get for a dime?   __try__

3. I want French _____fries_____ with my hamburger.   __fry__

4. He is invited to two _____parties_____ on the same day.   __party__

5. There are three large _____factories_____ in that part of town.   __factory__

6. Dad was in several _____countries_____ while he was in the Air Force.   __country__

7. That truck _____carries_____ over a ton of earth.   __carry__

8. His sister _____marries_____ in June.   __marry__

9. Helen and I picked _____berries_____ in the garden.   __berry__

10. My dog usually _____buries_____ his bones by the back door.   __bury__

11. The baby _____cries_____ when he is hungry.   __cry__

12. The hay _____dries_____ in the sun after it is cut.   __dry__

MASTERY REQUIREMENT: 9 correct responses

Indicate mastery on the student response sheet with a check.

II. WORD ANALYSIS

  A. Refine Phonics Skills

    3. Changes in words

      d. Changing <u>y</u> to <u>i</u> before
          adding <u>es</u>

Name _____

Date _____

Mastery _____

DIRECTIONS: Fill the blank in each sentence by using the correct form
             of the word at the end of the sentence.

1. My kite _____ better than yours does.   ___fly___

2. How many _____ do you get for a dime?   ___try___

3. I want French _____ with my hamburger.   ___fry___

4. He is invited to two _____ on the same day.   ___party___

5. There are three large _____ in that part
    of town.   ___factory___

6. Dad was in several _____ while he was in
    the Air Force.   ___country___

7. That truck _____ over a ton of earth.   ___carry___

8. His sister _____ in June.   ___marry___

9. Helen and I picked _____ in the garden.   ___berry___

10. My dog usually _____ his bones by the
    back door.   ___bury___

11. The baby _____ when he is hungry.   ___cry___

12. The hay _____ in the sun after it is
    cut.   ___dry___

II. WORD ANALYSIS   A. Refine Phonics Skills   4. Vowel rules

                                                 a. Vowel in one-syllable word
                                                    is short

OBJECTIVE: The student will identify vowels in one-syllable words as being short.

DIRECTIONS: Draw a circle around each word that contains a short vowel.

1. (pan)

2. before

3. (dip)

4. (run)

5. lately

6. pony

7. (bet)

8. croak

9. fireplace

10. (top)

MASTERY REQUIREMENT: 8 correct responses

Indicate mastery on the student response sheet with a check.

THIRD LEVEL

II. WORD ANALYSIS

Name _____

    A. Refine Phonics Skills

Date _____

        4. Vowel rules

           a. Vowel in one-syllable   Mastery _____
              word is short

DIRECTIONS: Draw a circle around each word that contains a short vowel.

    1. pan

    2. before

    3. dip

    4. run

    5. lately

    6. pony

    7. bet

    8. croak

    9. fireplace

    10. top

II. WORD ANALYSIS   A. Refine Phonics Skills   4. Vowel rules

b. **Vowel in word or syllable ending in e is long**

OBJECTIVE: The student will identify vowels in words or syllables ending in e as long.

DIRECTIONS: Draw a circle around each word that contains a long vowel.

1. (tape)

2. kin

3. (behave)

4. (cute)

5. (these)

6. (time)

7. tap

8. lot

9. pet

10. put

MASTERY REQUIREMENT: 8 correct responses

Indicate mastery on the student response sheet with a check.

THIRD LEVEL

II. WORD ANALYSIS

   A. Refine Phonics Skills

     4. Vowel rules

       b. Vowel in word or syllable ending in <u>e</u> is long

Name _____

Date _____

Mastery _____

DIRECTIONS: Draw a circle around each word that contains a long vowel.

1. tape

2. kin

3. behave

4. cute

5. these

6. time

7. tap

8. lot

9. pet

10. put

THIRD LEVEL

II.   WORD ANALYSIS   A.   Refine Phonics Skills   4.   Vowel rules

c.   Two vowels together

OBJECTIVE: The student will know that when two vowels are together, the first is often long and the second is silent.

DIRECTIONS: In the following words, underline the long vowels and draw a circle around the silent vowels.

1.   g   l   <u>e</u>   (a)   m

2.   b   <u>e</u>   (a)   m

3.   b   <u>o</u>   (a)   t

4.   t   <u>a</u>   (i)   l

5.   m   <u>a</u>   (i)   d

6.   f   <u>o</u>   (a)   m

7.   s   t   <u>e</u>   (a)   l

8.   c   l   <u>u</u>   (e)

9.   s   <u>o</u>   (a)   p

10. h   <u>e</u>   (a)   t

MASTERY REQUIREMENT: 8 correct responses

Indicate mastery on the student response sheet with a check.

II. WORD ANALYSIS

Name _____

A. Refine Phonics Skills

Date _____

4. Vowel rules

c. Two vowels together

Mastery _____

DIRECTIONS: In the following words, underline the long vowels and draw a circle around the silent vowels.

1. g l e a m

2. b e a m

3. b o a t

4. t a i l

5. m a i d

6. f o a m

7. s t e a l

8. c l u e

9. s o a p

10. h e a t

II. WORD ANALYSIS   A.   Refine Phonics Skills   4.   Vowel rules

d.   Vowel alone in word

OBJECTIVE: The student will know that a vowel alone in a word is usually short.

DIRECTIONS: Draw a circle around each of the following words that has a short vowel.

1. (man)

2. (pit)

3. mule

4. (let)

5. deed

6. mine

7. pane

8. (mop)

9. (pup)

10. pole

MASTERY REQUIREMENT: 9 correct responses

Indicate mastery on the student response sheet with a check.

THIRD LEVEL

II. WORD ANALYSIS

   A. Refine Phonics Skills

      4. Vowel rules

         d. Vowel alone in word

Name _____

Date _____

Mastery _____

DIRECTIONS: Draw a circle around each of the following words that has a short vowel.

1. man

2. pit

3. mule

4. let

5. deed

6. mine

7. pane

8. mop

9. pup

10. pole

© 1999 by The Center for Applied Research in Education, Inc.

II. WORD ANALYSIS   A. Refine Phonics Skills   5. Sounds of c

OBJECTIVE: The student will differentiate between conditions which cause c to have the s sound and the k sound.

DIRECTIONS: Circle the correct beginning sound for each of the following words. If you think the c would have the s sound, circle the s; if you think the c would make a k sound, circle the k.

1.	cellar	(s)	k
2.	calf	s	(k)
3.	coal	s	(k)
4.	call	s	(k)
5.	cold	s	(k)
6.	certain	(s)	k
7.	coat	s	(k)
8.	ceiling	(s)	k
9.	came	s	(k)
10.	cent	(s)	k
11.	cell	(s)	k
12.	cup	s	(k)

MASTERY REQUIREMENT: 9 correct responses

Indicate mastery on the student response sheet with a check.

II. WORD ANALYSIS

Name _____

   A. Refine Phonics Skills

Date _____

     5. Sounds of c

Mastery _____

DIRECTIONS: Circle the correct beginning sound for each of the following words. If you think the c would have the s sound, circle the s; if you think the c would make a k sound, circle the k.

1.	cellar	s	k
2.	calf	s	k
3.	coal	s	k
4.	call	s	k
5.	cold	s	k
6.	certain	s	k
7.	coat	s	k
8.	ceiling	s	k
9.	came	s	k
10.	cent	s	k
11.	cell	s	k
12.	cup	s	k

II.   WORD ANALYSIS   A.   Refine Phonics Skills   6.   Sounds of g

OBJECTIVE: The student will differentiate between conditions which cause g to have the j sound and the guh sound.

DIRECTIONS: Circle the correct beginning sound for each of the following words. If you think the g would have the j sound, circle the j after the word; if you think the g would have the guh sound, circle the guh after the word.

1.   gem   (j)   guh

2.   game   j   (guh)

3.   gate   j   (guh)

4.   gentle   (j)   guh

5.   goat   j   (guh)

6.   general   (j)   guh

7.   gum   j   (guh)

8.   gift   j   (guh)

9.   germ   (j)   guh

10.   girl   j   (guh)

MASTERY REQUIREMENT: 7 correct responses

Indicate mastery on the student response sheet with a check.

II. WORD ANALYSIS

    A. Refine Phonics Skills

        6. Sounds of g

Name _____

Date _____

Mastery _____

DIRECTIONS: Circle the correct beginning sound for each of the following words. If you think the g would have the j sound, circle the j after the word; if you think the g would have the guh sound, circle the guh after the word.

1. gem   j   guh

2. game   j   guh

3. gate   j   guh

4. gentle   j   guh

5. goat   j   guh

6. general   j   guh

7. gum   j   guh

8. gift   j   guh

9. germ   j   guh

10. girl   j   guh

THIRD LEVEL

II. WORD ANALYSIS   A. Refine Phonics Skills   7. Silent letters in <u>kn, wr, gn</u>

OBJECTIVE: The student will know the conditions that cause <u>k</u>, <u>w</u>, and <u>g</u> to be silent as initial letters.

DIRECTIONS: Here are twelve words beginning with consonant blends. Read each of these words to yourself and circle the silent consonant in each word.

1. (k) n o w

2. (w) r i t e

3. (g) n o m e

4. (w) r o n g

5. (k) n o t

6. (w) r e a t h

7. (g) n a w

8. (w) r i n g

9. (k) n o c k

10. (g) n a r l

11. (k) n i t

12. (w) r i s t

MASTERY REQUIREMENT: 9 correct responses

Indicate mastery on the student response sheet with a check.

II. WORD ANALYSIS

Name _____

Date _____

Mastery _____

    A. Refine Phonics Skills

        7. Silent letters in <u>kn,</u>
            <u>wr, gn</u>

DIRECTIONS: Here are twelve words beginning with consonant blends. Read each of these words to yourself and circle the silent consonant in each word.

1. k n o w

2. w r i t e

3. g n o m e

4. w r o n g

5. k n o t

6. w r e a t h

7. g n a w

8. w r i n g

9. k n o c k

10. g n a r l

11. k n i t

12. w r i s t

II. WORD ANALYSIS   B. Knows Skills   1. Forming plurals

a. Adding, <u>s</u>, <u>es</u>, <u>ies</u>

OBJECTIVE: The student will form plurals correctly by adding <u>s</u>, <u>es</u>, <u>ies</u>.

DIRECTIONS: Write the plural for each of these words.

1.	paper	papers
2.	book	books
3.	torch	torches
4.	rabbit	rabbits
5.	fox	foxes
6.	studio	studios
7.	college	colleges
8.	buzz	buzzes
9.	army	armies
10.	baby	babies
11.	match	matches
12.	puppy	puppies

MASTERY REQUIREMENT: 10 correct responses

Indicate mastery on the student response sheet with a check.

THIRD LEVEL

II. WORD ANALYSIS

    B. Knows Skills

        1. Forming plurals

           a. Adding <u>s</u>, <u>es</u>, <u>ies</u>

Name _____

Date _____

Mastery _____

DIRECTIONS: Write the plural for each of these words.

      1.   paper   _____

      2.   book   _____

      3.   torch   _____

      4.   rabbit   _____

      5.   fox   _____

      6.   studio   _____

      7.   college   _____

      8.   buzz   _____

      9.   army   _____

    10.   baby   _____

    11.   match   _____

    12.   puppy   _____

II.   WORD ANALYSIS   B.   Knows Skills   1.   Forming plurals

                                    b.   Changing <u>f</u> to <u>v</u> and adding <u>es</u>

OBJECTIVE: The student will form plurals correctly by changing <u>f</u> to <u>v</u> and adding <u>es</u>.

DIRECTIONS: Write the plurals for each of these words.

1.   self   selves

2.   wolf   wolves

3.   calf   calves

4.   knife   knives

5.   half   halves

6.   shelf   shelves

7.   wife   wives

8.   leaf   leaves

9.   thief   thieves

10.   scarf   scarves

MASTERY REQUIREMENT: 7 correct responses

Indicate mastery on the student response sheet with a check.

II. WORD ANALYSIS

    B. Knows Skills

        1. Forming plurals

           b. Changing f to v and adding es

Name _____

Date _____

Mastery _____

DIRECTIONS: Write the plurals for each of these words.

1. self   _____

2. wolf   _____

3. calf   _____

4. knife   _____

5. half   _____

6. shelf   _____

7. wife   _____

8. leaf   _____

9. thief   _____

10. scarf   _____

II. WORD ANALYSIS   B. Knows Skills   2. Similarities of sounds

OBJECTIVE: The student will know that different letter combinations may make similar sounds.

DIRECTIONS: For each word in the first column, find the word in the second column where the underlined letters make the same sound. Write the letter in the blank.

_d_	1.	t<u>oo</u>	a.	c<u>ur</u>led
_f_	2.	bo<u>x</u>	b.	blu<u>ff</u>ed
_a_	3.	w<u>or</u>ld	c.	gira<u>ff</u>e
_e_	4.	dr<u>ow</u>se	d.	bl<u>ew</u>
_b_	5.	tu<u>ft</u>	e.	pl<u>ow</u>s
_c_	6.	lau<u>gh</u>	f.	bl<u>ock</u>s

_c_	1.	tu<u>x</u>	a.	t<u>oa</u>d
_f_	2.	wr<u>i</u>te	b.	st<u>ea</u>k
_b_	3.	<u>a</u>che	c.	tru<u>ck</u>s
_a_	4.	exp<u>lo</u>de	d.	wi<u>n</u>ks
_d_	5.	mi<u>nx</u>	e.	sh<u>ow</u>n
_e_	6.	c<u>o</u>ne	f.	br<u>igh</u>t

MASTERY REQUIREMENT: 10 correct responses

Indicate mastery on the student response sheet with a check.

II. WORD ANALYSIS

    B. Knows Skills

       2. Similarities of sounds

Name _____

Date _____

Mastery _____

DIRECTIONS: For each word in the first column, find the word in the second column where the underlined letters make the same sound. Write the letter in the blank.

_____	1. t<u>oo</u>	a.	<u>c</u>urled
_____	2. bo<u>x</u>	b.	blu<u>ff</u>ed
_____	3. w<u>or</u>ld	c.	gira<u>ff</u>e
_____	4. dr<u>ow</u>se	d.	ble<u>w</u>
_____	5. tu<u>f</u>t	e.	pl<u>ow</u>s
_____	6. lau<u>gh</u>	f.	blo<u>cks</u>

_____	1. t<u>ux</u>	a.	<u>t</u>oad
_____	2. <u>wr</u>ite	b.	st<u>ea</u>k
_____	3. <u>a</u>che	c.	tr<u>u</u>cks
_____	4. explo<u>de</u>	d.	<u>w</u>inks
_____	5. mi<u>nx</u>	e.	sh<u>own</u>
_____	6. c<u>o</u>ne	f.	br<u>igh</u>t

THIRD LEVEL

II. WORD ANALYSIS   B. Knows Skills   3. Roman numerals

OBJECTIVE: The student will read the Roman numerals I, V, and X.

DIRECTIONS: Match the following by writing the correct letter in the blank.

    c   1. Five   a.   I

    a   2. One   b.   X

    b   3. Ten   c.   V

MASTERY REQUIREMENT: All correct

Indicate mastery on the student response sheet with a check.

II. WORD ANALYSIS

    B. Knows Skills

        3. Roman numerals

Name _____

Date _____

Mastery _____

DIRECTIONS: Match the following by writing the correct letter in the blank.

    _____ 1. Five   a.   I

    _____ 2. One   b.   X

    _____ 3. Ten   c.   V

II. WORD ANALYSIS   C. Syllabication   1. Usually as many syllables in word as there are vowels

OBJECTIVE: The student will know there are usually as many syllables in a word as there are vowels.

DIRECTIONS: How many syllables does each of the following words have? Write the number on the line next to each word.

1.	card	1
2.	storm	1
3.	mushroom	2
4.	trash	1
5.	zipper	2
6.	dream	1
7.	airplane	2
8.	dinner	2
9.	sidewalk	2
10.	basketball	3
11.	hamburger	3
12.	automobile	4

MASTERY REQUIREMENT: 10 correct responses

Indicate mastery on the student response sheet with a check.

II.   WORD ANALYSIS

   C.   Syllabication

      1.   Usually as many syllables
           in word as there are vowels

Name _____

Date _____

Mastery _____

DIRECTIONS: How many syllables does each of the following words
              have? Write the number on the line next to each word.

      1.   card   _____

      2.   storm   _____

      3.   mushroom   _____

      4.   trash   _____

      5.   zipper   _____

      6.   dream   _____

      7.   airplane   _____

      8.   dinner   _____

      9.   sidewalk   _____

      10. basketball   _____

      11. hamburger   _____

      12. automobile   _____

II. WORD ANALYSIS   C. Syllabication   2. Single consonant between two vowels

OBJECTIVE: The student will know that when a single consonant comes between two vowels, the vowel goes with the first syllable.

DIRECTIONS: Draw a line (/) in the following words where they should be divided into syllables.

    1. p u / p i l

    2. m i / n o r

    3. l a / t e x

    4. s e / r e n e

    5. r e / t i r e

    6. p a / t e n t

    7. c h o / r a l

    8. b a / g e l

    9. s t o / r y

    10. n a / v y

    11. p a / p e r

    12. c a / b l e

MASTERY REQUIREMENT: 9 correct responses

Indicate mastery on the student response sheet with a check.

II. WORD ANALYSIS

    C. Syllabication

        2. Single consonant between
            two vowels

Name _____

Date _____

Mastery _____

DIRECTIONS: Draw a line (/) in the following words where they should be divided into syllables.

    1. p u p i l

    2. m i n o r

    3. l a t e x

    4. s e r e n e

    5. r e t i r e

    6. p a t e n t

    7. c h o r a l

    8. b a g e l

    9. s t o r y

    10. n a v y

    11. p a p e r

    12. c a b l e

II. WORD ANALYSIS   C. Syllabication   3. Double consonants

OBJECTIVE: The student will know that in the case of double consonants, the syllable break comes between the two consonants.

DIRECTIONS: Draw a line (/) in the following words where you think they should be divided into syllables.

1. m i l / l e r

2. l i t / t l e

3. d o l / l y

4. f i d / d l e

5. n i b / b l e

6. a l / l e y

7. c a t / t l e

8. h i t / t e r

9. f l a n / n e l

10. c h a t / t e r

11. p u l / l e y

12. s e t / t l e r

MASTERY REQUIREMENT: 8 correct responses

Indicate mastery on the student response sheet with a check.

II. WORD ANALYSIS

    C. Syllabication

       3. Double consonants

Name _____

Date _____

Mastery _____

DIRECTIONS: Draw a line (/) in the following words where you think they should be divided into syllables.

    1. m i l l e r

    2. l i t t l e

    3. d o l l y

    4. f i d d l e

    5. n i b b l e

    6. a l l e y

    7. c a t t l e

    8. h i t t e r

    9. f l a n n e l

    10. c h a t t e r

    11. p u l l e y

    12. s e t t l e r

II.   WORD ANALYSIS   D.   Hyphenation of Words

OBJECTIVE: The student will hyphenate words correctly using syllable rules.

DIRECTIONS: Below are ten words. The second column shows each word continued from one line to the next. Some of the words are continued correctly and some are incorrect. Place a ($\sqrt{}$) by those that are correct and an ($\times$) by those that are incorrect.

1.	practical	prac- tical	$\sqrt{}$
2.	simple	sim- ple	$\sqrt{}$
3.	hornet	hor- net	$\sqrt{}$
4.	horrible	hor- rible	$\sqrt{}$
5.	spoon	spo- on	$\times$
6.	earring	ear- ring	$\sqrt{}$
7.	apiece	a- piece	$\sqrt{}$
8.	stucco	stucc- o	$\times$
9.	baked	bak- ed	$\times$
10.	slight	sli- ght	$\times$

MASTERY REQUIREMENT: 8 correct responses

Indicate mastery on the student response sheet with a check.

II.   **WORD ANALYSIS**

Name _____

D.   Hyphenation of Words

Date _____

Mastery _____

DIRECTIONS: Below are ten words. The second column shows each word continued from one line to the next. Some of the words are continued correctly and some are incorrect. Place a (√) by those that are correct and an (×) by those that are incorrect.

1.   practical   prac-
tical   _____

2.   simple   sim-
ple   _____

3.   hornet   hor-
net   _____

4.   horrible   hor-
rible   _____

5.   spoon   spo-
on   _____

6.   earring   ear-
ring   _____

7.   apiece   a-
piece   _____

8.   stucco   stucc-
o   _____

9.   baked   bak-
ed   _____

10.   slight   sli-
ght   _____

THIRD LEVEL

II. WORD ANALYSIS   E.   Primary Accent Mark

OBJECTIVE: The student will understand the use of the primary accent mark.

DIRECTIONS: Read the following words and underline the syllable that should receive the accent mark.

    1.   <u>mu</u>-sic

    2.   <u>oc</u>-to-pus

    3.   <u>dis</u>-tance

    4.   ma-<u>chine</u>

    5.   <u>veg</u>-e-ta-ble

    6.   tor-<u>ped</u>-o

    7.   <u>col</u>-o-ny

    8.   <u>sta</u>-tion

    9.   dis-<u>hon</u>-est

   10.   <u>ham</u>-bur-ger

   11.   ed-u-<u>ca</u>-tion

   12.   <u>mil</u>-i-tar-y

MASTERY REQUIREMENT: 9 correct responses

Indicate mastery on the student response sheet with a check.

II.   WORD ANALYSIS

     E.   Primary Accent Mark

Name _____

Date _____

Mastery _____

DIRECTIONS: Read the following words and underline the syllable that should receive the accent mark.

    1.   mu-sic

    2.   oc-to-pus

    3.   dis-tance

    4.   ma-chine

    5.   veg-e-ta-ble

    6.   tor-ped-o

    7.   col-o-ny

    8.   sta-tion

    9.   dis-hon-est

    10.   ham-bur-ger

    11.   ed-u-ca-tion

    12.   mil-i-tar-y

II. WORD ANALYSIS   F.   Accent First Syllable unless Prefix

OBJECTIVE: The student will know that the first syllable usually receives the accent unless it is a prefix.

DIRECTIONS: Underline the syllable which should receive the primary accent in these words.

    1. <u>gold</u>-en

    2. <u>cot</u>-ton

    3. re-<u>port</u>

    4. <u>lot</u>-te-ry

    5. <u>ho</u>-ly

    6. <u>ob</u>-vi-ous

    7. <u>skel</u>-e-ton

    8. un-<u>ti</u>-dy

    9. <u>ag</u>-o-ny

   10. be-<u>hind</u>

MASTERY REQUIREMENT: 9 correct responses

Indicate mastery on the student response sheet with a check.

II. WORD ANALYSIS

    F.   Accent First Syllable
          unless Prefix

Name _____

Date _____

Mastery _____

DIRECTIONS: Underline the syllable which should receive the primary accent in these words.

1.   gold-en

2.   cot-ton

3.   re-port

4.   lot-te-ry

5.   ho-ly

6.   ob-vi-ous

7.   skel-e-ton

8.   un-ti-dy

9.   ag-o-ny

10.   be-hind

THIRD LEVEL

III. COMPREHENSION   A. Main Idea

OBJECTIVE: The student will be able to find the main idea in a story.

DIRECTIONS: Read this story, then answer the question below.

Do you know what a cacao is? A cacao is a large, yellow fruit. This fruit grows quite large—sometimes as much as eight or nine inches long. It is filled with many seeds about the size of large peanuts. These seeds are used to make a kind of candy most children like very much. The tree on which the cacao fruit grows is found in the warm, wet countries of South and Central America. The workers on the farms that grow cacao watch the fruit very closely to know when it is ripe. At just the right time, the seeds are taken out, cleaned, and roasted. After they have roasted just enough, they are mashed into a paste. Sugar and vanilla are added to the paste. The paste is then spread out in thin sheets to dry. After it has hardened enough, it is cut into bars and wrapped. Do you know what it is yet? Right! Chocolate bars!

What is this story about?

_____   1.   How to grow a cacao tree

  X   2.   How a chocolate bar is made

_____   3.   Plants that grow in warm countries

_____   4.   The kinds of candy that are made
              from chocolate bars

MASTERY REQUIREMENT: Correct response

Indicate mastery on the student response sheet with a check.

III. COMPREHENSION

    A.   Main Idea

Name _____

Date _____

Mastery _____

DIRECTIONS: Read this story, then answer the question below.

Do you know what a cacao is? A cacao is a large, yellow fruit. This fruit grows quite large—sometimes as much as eight or nine inches long. It is filled with many seeds about the size of large peanuts. These seeds are used to make a kind of candy most children like very much. The tree on which the cacao fruit grows is found in the warm, wet countries of South and Central America. The workers on the farms that grow cacao watch the fruit very closely to know when it is ripe. At just the right time, the seeds are taken out, cleaned, and roasted. After they have roasted just enough, they are mashed into a paste. Sugar and vanilla are added to the paste. The paste is then spread out in thin sheets to dry. After it has hardened enough, it is cut into bars and wrapped. Do you know what it is yet? Right! Chocolate bars!

What is this story about?

_____ 1.   How to grow a cacao tree

_____ 2.   How a chocolate bar is made

_____ 3.   Plants that grow in warm countries

_____ 4.   The kinds of candy that are made from chocolate bars

III. COMPREHENSION   B.   Sequence of Events

OBJECTIVE: The student will keep events in a story in proper sequence.

DIRECTIONS: Read this story, then try to answer the questions below without looking back at the story.

Kay Baker and her dad put in a full day of work on Saturday fencing in the back yard. Then Sunday afternoon they worked until nearly dark building a doghouse. Now Prince had a safe place to play and a dry place to sleep.

Kay found an article in a book about dogs like Prince. He was a German Shepherd. They make good playmates for children, but are also excellent watchdogs and fighters when they need to be.

Prince is small now because he is just a puppy. He can almost crawl through the fence. When he grows up, though, he will be a large dog. Some German Shepherds weigh as much as a hundred pounds. He will be a good pet and also a useful and brave watchdog.

1. When did the Baker family get Prince?

    _____   a.   When they saw how he could fight.

    _____   b.   When he was grown.

    __X__   c.   When he was little.

2. The first night Prince could sleep in his new doghouse was

    _____   a.   Saturday.

    __X__   b.   Sunday.

3. According to the story, Kay and her dad finished working

    _____   a.   Saturday morning.

    _____   b.   Saturday afternoon.

    _____   c.   Sunday morning.

    __X__   d.   Sunday afternoon.

MASTERY REQUIREMENT: All correct

Indicate mastery on the student response sheet with a check.

THIRD LEVEL

III. COMPREHENSION

B. Sequence of Events

Name _____

Date _____

Mastery _____

DIRECTIONS: Read this story, then try to answer the questions below without looking back at the story.

Kay Baker and her dad put in a full day of work on Saturday fencing in the back yard. Then Sunday afternoon they worked until nearly dark building a doghouse. Now Prince had a safe place to play and a dry place to sleep.

Kay found an article in a book about dogs like Prince. He was a German Shepherd. They make good playmates for children, but are also excellent watchdogs and fighters when they need to be.

Prince is small now because he is just a puppy. He can almost crawl through the fence. When he grows up, though, he will be a large dog. Some German Shepherds weigh as much as a hundred pounds. He will be a good pet and also a useful and brave watchdog.

1. When did the Baker family get Prince?

_____ a. When they saw how he could fight.

_____ b. When he was grown.

_____ c. When he was little.

2. The first night Prince could sleep in his new doghouse was

_____ a. Saturday

_____ b. Sunday

3. According to the story, Kay and her dad finished working

_____ a. Saturday morning.

_____ b. Saturday afternoon.

_____ c. Sunday morning.

_____ d. Sunday afternoon.

© 1999 by The Center for Applied Research in Education, Inc.

III. COMPREHENSION   C. Can Draw Logical Conclusions

OBJECTIVE: The student will draw logical conclusions.

DIRECTIONS: Read this story, then answer the question that follows it.

"We need to stop soon for gasoline," Dad said as we neared the town where Grandmother lived. "Look, the needle is on empty. Maybe we can make it to her house. If we can, we'll get gas when we leave."

We drove on and, sure enough, we made it to Grandmother's house without running out of gas. We stayed and stayed. We stayed much longer than we had intended to. In fact, it was nearly midnight when we started getting ready to leave.

Suddenly Dad exclaimed, "You know, we may have a problem. It is a lot later than I thought we would be leaving."

Why is Dad worried about how late it is?   <u>Lateness may make it difficult to find an open gas station.</u>

MASTERY REQUIREMENT: Correct response

Indicate mastery on the student response sheet with a check.

III. **COMPREHENSION**

    C. **Can Draw Logical
Conclusions**

Name _____

Date _____

Mastery _____

DIRECTIONS: Read this story, then answer the question that follows it.

"We need to stop soon for gasoline," Dad said as we neared the town where Grandmother lived. "Look, the needle is on empty. Maybe we can make it to her house. If we can, we'll get gas when we leave."

We drove on and, sure enough, we made it to Grandmother's house without running out of gas. We stayed and stayed. We stayed much longer than we had intended to. In fact, it was nearly midnight when we started getting ready to leave.

Suddenly Dad exclaimed, "You know, we may have a problem. It is a lot later than I thought we would be leaving."

Why is Dad worried about how late it is? _____

_____

III. COMPREHENSION D. Can See Relationships

OBJECTIVE: The student will be able to see relationships.

DIRECTIONS: Mark the *best* choice for each of the following.

1. One of the nice things trees do for us is give shade. It is very pleasant to rest in the shade of a tree on a

    _____ a. cloudy day.

    _____ b. cool day.

    __X__ c. hot day.

2. It is dark in here. Will you please turn on the

    _____ a. radio.

    __X__ b. light.

    _____ c. water.

3. "I guess we must be lost," Mom said. "I don't know which road to take at this corner." Dad suggested that we pull over and look at

    _____ a. the car.

    _____ b. the light.

    __X__ c. the map.

4. "Hurry, Bob, or we are going to be

    __X__ a. late."

    _____ b. tired."

    _____ c. angry."

MASTERY REQUIREMENT: All correct

Indicate mastery on the student response sheet with a check.

III. COMPREHENSION

   D. Can See Relationships

© 1999 by The Center for Applied Research in Education, Inc.

Name _____

Date _____

Mastery _____

DIRECTIONS: Mark the *best* choice for each of the following.

1. One of the nice things trees do for us is give shade. It is very pleasant to rest in the shade of a tree on a

   _____ a. cloudy day.

   _____ b. cool day.

   _____ c. hot day.

2. It is dark in here. Will you please turn on the

   _____ a. radio.

   _____ b. light.

   _____ c. water.

3. "I guess we must be lost," Mom said. "I don't know which road to take at this corner." Dad suggested that we pull over and look at

   _____ a. the car.

   _____ b. the light.

   _____ c. the map.

4. "Hurry, Bob, or we are going to be

   _____ a. late."

   _____ b. tired."

   _____ c. angry."

III. COMPREHENSION   E.   Can Predict Outcomes

OBJECTIVE: The student will be able to predict outcomes.

DIRECTIONS: Read the two short stories on this page, then write your own ending to each story.

Beth was tired. She had run all the way to the bus stop because she was afraid she was going to miss her school bus. When she got there the bus was not even in sight. "Whew!" she panted, "I'm glad I can rest here on the bench for a little while." She sat down on the bench, not noticing how bright and shiny it looked.

(After she had been seated for a little while, she felt something funny. She was sort of sticking to

the bench. Suddenly she saw a sign on the back of the bench. The sign said, WET PAINT.)

Frank was happy to receive a ten dollar bill from his uncle as a birthday present. For days, he thought about what to buy with the money. Finally, he decided to buy a game he saw advertised in the newspaper. Frank put the ten dollar bill into the pocket of his old jacket when his mother said they were ready to go shopping.

(At the store, Frank found the game he wanted and took it to the counter to pay for it. When he

reached into his pocket for the money, he was shocked to find that the pocket had a hole in it

and the ten dollar bill was not there.)

MASTERY REQUIREMENT: Teacher judgment (This is an open-ended exercise. Any answer the student writes that makes sense is acceptable.)

Indicate mastery on the student response sheet with a check.

THIRD LEVEL

III. COMPREHENSION

    E. Can Predict Outcomes

Name _____

Date _____

Mastery _____

DIRECTIONS: Read the two short stories on this page, then write your own ending to each story.

    Beth was tired. She had run all the way to the bus stop because she was afraid she was going to miss her school bus. When she got there the bus was not even in sight. "Whew!" she panted, "I'm glad I can rest here on the bench for a little while." She sat down on the bench, not noticing how bright and shiny it looked.

_____

_____

_____

_____

    Frank was happy to receive a ten dollar bill from his uncle as a birthday present. For days, he thought about what to buy with the money. Finally, he decided to buy a game he saw advertised in the newspaper. Frank put the ten dollar bill into the pocket of his old jacket when his mother said they were ready to go shopping.

_____

_____

_____

III. COMPREHENSION   F.   Following Printed Directions

OBJECTIVE: The student can follow printed directions.

DIRECTIONS: 1. Draw a circle around all the capital vowels.

2. Underline the first and last letters in the row of small letters.

3. Draw a circle around the 4th, 7th, and 8th letters in the bottom row.

4. In these blanks, write words which begin with the middle or center letter in each row.

_____(word beginning with a   g)_____

_____(word beginning with a   t)_____

Ⓐ   B   C   D   Ⓔ   F   G   H   Ⓘ   J   K   L   M

<u>n</u>   o   p   ⓠ   r   s   ⓣ   ⓤ   v   w   x   y   <u>z</u>

MASTERY REQUIREMENT: All correct

Indicate mastery on the student response sheet with a check.

THIRD LEVEL

III. COMPREHENSION

Name _____

F. Following Printed
   Directions

Date _____

Mastery _____

DIRECTIONS: 1.   Draw a circle around all the capital vowels.

2.   Underline the first and last letters in the row of small letters.

3.   Draw a circle around the 4th, 7th, and 8th letters in the bottom row.

4.   In these blanks, write words which begin with the middle or center letter in each row.

_____

_____

A   B   C   D   E   F   G   H   I   J   K   L   M

n   o   p   q   r   s   t   u   v   w   x   y   z

III. COMPREHENSION   G.   Definite Purpose   1.   Pleasure

OBJECTIVE: The student reads for pleasure.

DIRECTIONS:

Ask the student to recall a story in a magazine or a novel which he or she has read with enjoyment recently. Do this periodically, insuring each time that the reading reported is not reading done in connection with a school assignment, but reading selected voluntarily and for pleasure.

MASTERY REQUIREMENT: Evidence that student reads for pleasure

Indicate mastery on the student response sheet with a check.

THIRD LEVEL

III. COMPREHENSION

    G. Definite Purpose

        1. Pleasure

Name _____

Date _____

Mastery _____

Comment: _____

_____

THIRD LEVEL

III. COMPREHENSION   G. Definite Purpose   2. Answer question

OBJECTIVE: The student will read for the purpose of obtaining an answer to a question.

DIRECTIONS: Write a question in the blank on the student response sheet. Ask the student to
               read some source (you may suggest some sources that you know are available)
               where the answer will be found and answer the question on the sheet.

               Suggestions: What kind of wood is used in making baseball bats?

                             Where do most of the diamonds in the world come from?

                             What was the first college in the United States?

                             What is the difference between horses and mules?

MASTERY REQUIREMENT: Obtaining an answer to the question assigned

Indicate mastery on the student response sheet with a check.

THIRD LEVEL

III. COMPREHENSION

    G. Definite Purpose

        2. Answer question

Name _____

Date _____

Mastery _____

Question: _____

_____

Answer: _____

_____

_____

Source of Answer: _____

_____

Teacher Comment: _____

_____

III.   COMPREHENSION   G.   Definite Purpose   3.   General idea of content

OBJECTIVE: The student will be able to read to obtain a general idea of content.

DIRECTIONS: Select short to medium-length articles from newspapers, magazines, elementary encylopedias, etc. Hand the article to the student. Vary them frequently to avoid familiarity.

SAY: You will not have enough time to read this word for word. Just scan through it long enough to find out what it is about and some of the most important things it says.

Give the student about one-fourth of the time that would be necessary to read the entire selection in detail.

SAY: Now stop and tell me what you know about the article you looked at.

MASTERY REQUIREMENT: Teacher judgment of ability to relate general content

Indicate mastery on the student response sheet with a check.

THIRD LEVEL

III. COMPREHENSION

    G. Definite Purpose

        3. General idea of content

Name _____

Date _____

Mastery _____

Comment: _____

_____

THIRD LEVEL

III. COMPREHENSION   H.   Classify Items

OBJECTIVE: The student will classify items into appropriate categories.

DIRECTIONS: Some of the things in this list are necessary for you to have in order to live. Others are pleasant or good to have, but not necessary for life. Write them in the proper column.

		Necessary	Good to Have
1.	books		books
2.	air	air	
3.	food	food	
4.	dog		dog
5.	bicycle		bicycle
6.	water	water	
7.	toys		toys

DIRECTIONS: Here is a list of foods. Think of two columns you can make from the list. Put a heading on the top line above each column, then write each food item in the proper column.

		Meats	Vegetables
1.	pork chop	pork chop	
2.	spinach		spinach
3.	drumstick	drumstick	
4.	steak	steak	
5.	asparagus		asparagus
6.	sausage	sausage	
7.	cabbage		cabbage
8.	bacon	bacon	

MASTERY REQUIREMENT: All correct

Indicate mastery on the student response sheet with a check.

III. COMPREHENSION

Name _____

H. Classify Items

Date _____

Mastery _____

DIRECTIONS: Some of the things in this list are necessary for you to have in order to live. Others are pleasant or good to have, but not necessary for life. Write them in the proper column.

	Necessary	Good to Have
1. books	_____	_____
2. air	_____	_____
3. food	_____	_____
4. dog	_____	_____
5. bicycle	_____	_____
6. water	_____	_____
7. toys	_____	_____

DIRECTIONS: Here is a list of foods. Think of two columns you can make from the list. Put a heading on the top line above each column, then write each food item in the proper column.

	_____	_____
1. pork chop	_____	_____
2. spinach	_____	_____
3. drumstick	_____	_____
4. steak	_____	_____
5. asparagus	_____	_____
6. sausage	_____	_____
7. cabbage	_____	_____
8. bacon	_____	_____

THIRD LEVEL

III. COMPREHENSION   I.   Use of Index

OBJECTIVE: The student will know how to use an index.

DIRECTIONS: Write TRUE or FALSE by each of these statements.

     false   1.   The index is usually near the front of the book.

     true   2.   The index lists items in alphabetical order.

     true   3.   The index lists all pages on which a topic is mentioned.

     false   4.   The index lists the title of each chapter.

     false   5.   The index lists items in order of page number.

     true   6.   The index is near the back of the book.

Use this short index to a health book to answer the questions below:

Accident prevention, 59-60, 85, 141-
    143, 224-225

Blood
    Amount in body, 215
    Circulation of, 56, 75-77, 162, 194

Bones
    Growth of, 120-121, 244-245
    In skeleton, 108, 110

Breathing
    How you breathe, 113, 208-210

Hands
    Bones of, 112

Hearing, sense of, 23, 24, 27, 37-38
Heart
    Care of, 132, 198, 216

Safety
    Avoiding burns, 85
    Avoiding falls, 141-143
Senses (see Hearing, Sight, Smell,
    Taste, Touch)
Sight, sense of, 23, 24, 26, 28-30
Smell, sense of, 23, 24, 27, 44-46

Taste, sense of, 18, 23, 24, 27, 44
Touch, sense of, 23, 24, 27, 48

1.   On what page would you look to find how many pints
    of blood are in your body?   215

2.   How many pages would you need to read to find out
    all about your ears and how they work?   5

3.   How many pages tell you about how to avoid hurting
    yourself by accidentally falling?   3

4.   On what page would you look to find out about the
    bones in your hands?   112

5.   What page would tell you how to avoid burns?   85

6.   How many pages tell you about how you breathe?   4

MASTERY REQUIREMENT: 4 correct responses in each grouping of 6 questions

Indicate mastery on the student response sheet with a check.

III. COMPREHENSION

Name _____

    I. Use of Index

Date _____

Mastery _____

DIRECTIONS: Write TRUE or FALSE by each of these statements.

_____ 1. The index is usually near the front of the book.

_____ 2. The index lists items in alphabetical order.

_____ 3. The index lists all pages on which a topic is mentioned.

_____ 4. The index lists the title of each chapter.

_____ 5. The index lists items in order of page number.

_____ 6. The index is near the back of the book.

Use this short index to a health book to answer the questions below:

Accident prevention, 59-60, 85, 141-
   143, 224-225
Blood
   Amount in body, 215
   Circulation of, 56, 75-77, 162, 194
Bones
   Growth of, 120-121, 244-245
   In skeleton, 108, 110
Breathing
   How you breathe, 113, 208-210
Hands
   Bones of, 112

Hearing, sense of, 23, 24, 27, 37-38
Heart
   Care of, 132, 198, 216
Safety
   Avoiding burns, 85
   Avoiding falls, 141-143
Senses (see Hearing, Sight, Smell,
   Taste, Touch)
Sight, sense of, 23, 24, 26, 28-30
Smell, sense of, 23, 24, 27, 44-46
Taste, sense of, 18, 23, 24, 27, 44
Touch, sense of, 23, 24, 27, 48

1. On what page would you look to find how many pints of blood are in your body? _____

2. How many pages would you need to read to find out all about your ears and how they work? _____

3. How many pages tell you about how to avoid hurting yourself by accidentally falling? _____

4. On what page would you look to find out about the bones in your hands? _____

5. What page would tell you about how to avoid burns? _____

6. How many pages tell you about how you breathe? _____

III. COMPREHENSION   J. Alphabetizing (2-letter)

OBJECTIVE: The student will alphabetize words using two-letter discrimination.

DIRECTIONS: Write these words in alphabetical order in the second column.

1.	seltzer	amorous
2.	migrant	awkward
3.	awkward	epic
4.	filch	filch
5.	symptom	formicary
6.	zinc	harpy
7.	xylem	migrant
8.	amorous	penguin
9.	epic	seltzer
10.	harpy	symptom
11.	zany	xylem
12.	formicary	zany
13.	penguin	zinc

MASTERY REQUIREMENT: All correct

Indicate mastery on the student response sheet with a check.

III. **COMPREHENSION**

 J. **Alphabetizing (2-letter)**

Name _____

Date _____

Mastery _____

DIRECTIONS: Write these words in alphabetical order in the second column.

1. seltzer   _____

2. migrant   _____

3. awkward   _____

4. filch   _____

5. symptom   _____

6. zinc   _____

7. xylem   _____

8. amorous   _____

9. epic   _____

10. harpy   _____

11. zany   _____

12. formicary   _____

13. penguin   _____

III. COMPREHENSION   K.   Skimming

OBJECTIVE: The student will know the technique of skimming.

DIRECTIONS: Make a copy of the student response sheet and direct the student as follows.

SAY: I am going to hand you a sheet of paper face down. When I say GO, turn it over and follow the directions at the top of the page just as quickly as you can.

STUDENT DIRECTIONS: Read these paragraphs as quickly as you can, then answer the two questions about them.

In the early history of the West, buffalo meat was an important food for both the settlers and the Indians. Many buffalo roamed over the country in large herds. But as more settlers came and more buffalo were killed for food, the buffalo herds became smaller and smaller. At last there were only a few small herds left.

Then some people began to raise buffalo. Today, buffalo are raised on ranches in the same way as cattle. Some stores sell buffalo steaks, roasts, and ground meat. Many people think buffalo meat tastes just like beef. In some parts of the country, there are restaurants that serve special dishes made of buffalo meat. There is even a buffalo cookbook.

1. Who ate buffalo meat in the early West?   _____ settlers _____

     _____ Indians _____

2. What does buffalo meat taste like?   _____ beef _____

MASTERY REQUIREMENT: Completion in less than 30 seconds

Indicate mastery on the student response sheet with a check.

III. COMPREHENSION

   K. Skimming

Name _____

Date _____

Mastery _____

DIRECTIONS: Read these paragraphs as quickly as you can, then answer the two questions about them.

In the early history of the West, buffalo meat was an important food for both the settlers and the Indians. Many buffalo roamed over the country in large herds. But as more settlers came and more buffalo were killed for food, the buffalo herds became smaller and smaller. At last there were only a few small herds left.

Then some people began to raise buffalo. Today, buffalo are raised on ranches in the same way as cattle. Some stores sell buffalo steaks, roasts, and ground meat. Many people think buffalo meat tastes just like beef. In some parts of the country, there are restaurants that serve special dishes made of buffalo meat. There is even a buffalo cookbook.

1. Who ate buffalo meat in the
    early West?   _____

                                                 _____

2. What does buffalo meat taste
    like?   _____

III. COMPREHENSION   L.   Sources of Information

OBJECTIVE: The student will correctly choose the most efficient source to find various types of information.

DIRECTIONS: You have the following items in which to find information:

1. Dictionary
2. Encyclopedia
3. Today's newspaper
4. Almanac
5. Road map

A science book with a
6. Glossary
7. Index

Which of these would be the best place to look first for the following information? Write the number in the blank.

a.	Is there likely to be rain tomorrow?	3
b.	The life story of Ben Franklin	2
c.	The meaning of an unfamiliar word you find in your science lesson	6 or 1
d.	The towns you go through traveling from Madison to Clinton	5
e.	Information about blood pressure written in words you can understand	7
f.	The batting champion of the National League in 1954	4
g.	What the word "amphibian" means	1
h.	What science experiments were perfected by Madame Curie?	2
i.	The distance from Missouri to New Mexico	5
j.	What special sales are ongoing at the grocery store?	3

MASTERY REQUIREMENT: 8 correct responses

Indicate mastery on the student response sheet with a check.

THIRD LEVEL

III. COMPREHENSION

    L. Sources of Information

DIRECTIONS: You have the following items in which to find information.

    1. Dictionary
    2. Encyclopedia
    3. Today's newspaper
    4. Almanac
    5. Road map

A science book with a
    6. Glossary
    7. Index

Which of these would be the <u>best</u> place to look first for the following information? Write the number in the blank.

a. Is there likely to be rain tomorrow? _____

b. The life story of Ben Franklin _____

c. The meaning of an unfamiliar word you find in your science lesson _____

d. The towns you go through traveling from Madison to Clinton _____

e. Information about blood pressure written in words you can understand _____

f. The batting champion of the National League in 1954 _____

g. What the word "amphibian" means _____

h. What science experiments were perfected by Madame Curie? _____

i. The distance from Missouri to New Mexico _____

j. What special sales are ongoing at the grocery store? _____

III.   COMPREHENSION   M.   Use of Maps and Charts

OBJECTIVE: The student will use maps and charts.

DIRECTIONS: Secure several copies of road maps of your state. Hand a map to the student.

SAY: 1.   Show me our town on the map.

2.   Show me the capital of our state on the map.

3.   Show me the difference in the numbers on the map that show distance and the ones that are state and US highway numbers. (Refer the student to the legend for help, if needed.)

4.   What neighboring state do we live closest to?

5.   What highway would we get on to go there and what direction would we go?

6.   Show me how we can get an idea of how large a city is by looking at the map.

7.   Now turn to the highway mileage chart. Tell me how many miles it is from _____ to _____. (Be sure you are using towns listed on the chart.)

MASTERY REQUIREMENT: 5 correct responses

Indicate mastery on the student response sheet with a check.

III. COMPREHENSION

    M. Use of Maps and Charts

Name _____

Date _____

Mastery _____

Check successful responses:

_____ 1. Our town

_____ 2. Capital

_____ 3. Distance and highway numbers

_____ 4. Neighboring state

_____ 5. Highway number and direction

_____ 6. Size of cities

_____ 7. Mileage chart

IV. ORAL AND SILENT READING   A. Oral Reading   1. Reads with expression

OBJECTIVE: The student will read with expression.

DIRECTIONS: Read this story aloud.

"Isn't that something unlucky, now!" Becky complained. "I spent all my homework time last night working on this long page of math problems. Look! There are forty problems on the page, and I struggled through every one of them. Why, I didn't even get any help from mother! And now, after I get to school today, what happens? Joe tells me we were supposed to work page 95 in the workbook, not the textbook. Oh! That is disgusting. The workbook page we were supposed to do had six little problems on it. I could have watched my favorite TV program instead of spending all that time on my homework."

MASTERY REQUIREMENT: A rating of "Fair" or better (Teacher judgment)

Indicate mastery on the student response sheet with a check.

IV. ORAL AND SILENT READING

A. Oral Reading

1. Reads with expression

Name _____

Date _____

Mastery _____

DIRECTIONS: Read this story aloud.

"Isn't that something unlucky, now!" Becky complained. "I spent all my home-work time last night working on this long page of math problems. Look! There are forty problems on the page, and I struggled through every one of them. Why, I didn't even get any help from mother! And now, after I get to school today, what happens? Joe tells me we were supposed to work page 95 in the workbook, not the textbook. Oh! That is disgusting. The workbook page we were supposed to do had six little problems on it. I could have watched my favorite TV program instead of spending all that time on my homework."

Teacher rating: _____ Excellent

_____ Good

_____ Fair

_____ Poor

Comment: _____

IV. ORAL AND SILENT READING   A. Oral Reading   2. Comprehends material read aloud

OBJECTIVE: The student will comprehend material read aloud.

DIRECTIONS: Make a copy of the reading selection on the following page, hand the sheet to the student, and have the student return the sheet to you after he/she has read the passage.

STUDENT DIRECTIONS: Read this paragraph aloud.

Do you know anyone who has hay fever? From the name of this ailment, you might think it causes people who have it to have fever. This is not usually true. Although it causes many problems, very seldom is fever one of them. Hay fever is what is called an allergy. People who have it are allergic to the pollen that is produced by some kinds of plants. Because of this, they usually are affected about the same season of the year each year. When they breathe air with pollen in it, they sneeze, their nose gets runny, and their eyes water and stay red and itchy. Luckily, for most people these conditions last only a short time each year.

(Continued on page 130.)

DIRECTIONS: Read this paragraph aloud.

Do you know anyone who has hay fever? From the name of this ailment, you might think it causes people who have it to have fever. This is not usually true. Although it causes many problems, very seldom is fever one of them. Hay fever is what is called an allergy. People who have it are allergic to the pollen that is produced by some kinds of plants. Because of this, they usually are affected about the same season of the year each year. When they breathe air with pollen in it, they sneeze, their nose gets runny, and their eyes water and stay red and itchy. Luckily, for most people these conditions last only a short time each year.

DIRECTIONS: After obtaining the reading passage from the student, give the student the student response sheet.

STUDENT DIRECTIONS: Answer these questions about the passage you just read.

1. Does hay fever get its name because it causes most people to have high fever? _____no_____

2. Are most people who have hay fever bothered by it all year? _____no_____

3. When people with hay fever breathe air with pollen in it, what does it do to them? __causes sneezing, runny nose, watery eyes, red eyes, itching eyes.__

MASTERY REQUIREMENT: Correct responses on Nos. 1 and 2; at least two conditions named on No. 3

Indicate mastery on the student response sheet with a check.

IV. ORAL AND SILENT READING

A. Oral Reading

    2. Comprehends material
       read aloud

Name _____

Date _____

Mastery _____

DIRECTIONS: Answer these questions about the passage you just read.

1. Does hay fever get its name because it causes most people to have high
fever? _____

2. Are most people who have hay fever bothered by it all year? _____

3. When people with hay fever breathe air with pollen in it, what does it
do to them? _____

_____

THIRD LEVEL

IV. ORAL AND SILENT READING   B. Silent Reading   1. Finger pointing and lip
                                                                   movements

OBJECTIVE: The student will read silently without finger pointing or lip movement.

DIRECTIONS: Use any daily opportunities to appraise students on this objective. The ap-
              praisal should be made at a time when the student is unaware of being watched.

MASTERY REQUIREMENT: Demonstrated absence of mannerisms being appraised

Indicate mastery on the student response sheet with a check.

IV.   **ORAL AND SILENT READING**

    B.   **Silent Reading**

        1.   **Finger pointing and lip
            movement**

Name _____

Date _____

Mastery _____

Comment: _____

_____

_____

IV. ORAL AND SILENT READING   B. Silent Reading   2. Comprehends material
read silently

OBJECTIVE: The student will comprehend material which has been read silently.

DIRECTIONS: Hand the student a copy of the following passage, page 135, then have the student return it to you after he/she has read the passage.

Do you get confused about the difference between a microscope and a telescope? A microscope is used to make tiny things appear larger so we can study them in more detail and see things about them that we cannot see without the microscope. For example, a microscope can help us see tiny sea animals, the tiny cells which make up our bodies, and the beautiful designs of snowflakes.

A telescope is used to look at things that are a long way from us. It makes far-off things look as if they are very near. Using a telescope, scientists can study the moon, planets, and other bodies in space. Field glasses, or binoculars, that we use for seeing distant things here on earth are two telescopes mounted together.

Perhaps we can remember the difference between a microscope and a telescope if we learn the meanings of two prefixes: "micro" means very, very small; "tele" means far, far away.

(Continued on page 136.)

DIRECTIONS: Read this silently.

Do you get confused about the difference between a microscope and a telescope? A microscope is used to make tiny things appear larger so we can study them in more detail and see things about them that we cannot see without the microscope. For example, a microscope can help us see tiny sea animals, the tiny cells which make up our bodies, and the beautiful designs of snowflakes.

A telescope is used to look at things that are a long way from us. It makes far-off things look as if they are very near. Using a telescope, scientists can study the moon, planets, and other bodies in space. Field glasses, or binoculars, that we use for seeing distant things here on earth are two telescopes mounted together.

Perhaps we can remember the difference between a microscope and a telescope if we learn the meanings of two prefixes: "micro" means very, very small; "tele" means far, far away.

DIRECTIONS: After obtaining the reading passage from the student, give him/her the student response sheet with the following questions.

1.   If you wanted to examine a grain of sand very closely, would you use a telescope or a microscope? ____microscope____

2.   Would you need a microscope or a telescope if you wanted to get a better look at the moon? ____telescope____

3.   What are field glasses, or binoculars, made of? ____telescopes____

4.   If you wanted to look at the colors of the planet Mars, would you use a microscope or telescope? ____telescope____

5.   Would you use a microscope or a telescope if you were studying the tiny cells that make up the human body? ____microscope____

6.   What does the prefix "micro" mean? ____very small (or similar answer)____

7.   What does the prefix "tele" mean? ____far away (or similar answer)____

MASTERY REQUIREMENT: 5 correct responses

Indicate mastery on the student response sheet with a check.

IV. ORAL AND SILENT READING   Name _____

   B.   Silent Reading
                                       Date_____
      2.   Comprehends material
           read silently
                                       Mastery _____

DIRECTIONS: Answer these questions about the passage you just read.

1.   If you wanted to examine a grain of sand very closely, would you use a

     telescope or a microscope? _____

2.   Would you need a microscope or a telescope if you wanted to get a

     better look at the moon? _____

3.   What are field glasses, or binoculars, made of? _____

4.   If you wanted to look at the colors of the planet Mars, would you use a

     microscope or telescope? _____

5.   Would you need a telescope or a microscope if you were studying the

     tiny cells that make up the human body? _____

6.   What does the prefix "micro"mean? _____

7.   What does the prefix '"tele" mean? _____

IV.   ORAL AND SILENT READING   B.   Silent Reading   3.   **Reads faster silently than orally**

OBJECTIVE: The student will be able to read more rapidly silently than orally.

DIRECTIONS: Use an opportunity during a daily silent reading assignment to time the student in his silent reading of a page containing no pictures. The student should not be aware that an observation is occurring. Record the time between page turning on the student response sheet. At another time, have the student read orally from a page in the same book that also has no pictures, timing this reading. Likewise, record this time on the student response sheet.

MASTERY REQUIREMENT: Silent reading time shorter than oral

Indicate mastery on the student response sheet with a check.

IV. **ORAL AND SILENT READING**

    B. **Silent Reading**

        3. **Reads faster silently than orally**

Name _____

Date _____

Mastery _____

Number of seconds to read page orally   _____

Number of seconds to read page silently   _____

IV.   ORAL AND SILENT READING   C.   Listening   1.   Comprehends material read
by another

OBJECTIVE: The student will comprehend material read aloud by another.

DIRECTIONS: Listen as this is read aloud.

Is there an empty feeling in your school? Is something missing? We hope so because the Instructional Television Office has picked up the black-and-white television cameras from every school. These are going to be sold and the money used to purchase new color cameras.

Information about the color cameras, how they can be checked out, and how to use them, will be in your hands shortly.

Just as a word of early information—the color cameras will be light and easy to operate. However, they will only be available for three days at a time. A few black-and-white cameras will be retained to check out for extended periods of time.

Now answer the questions on your sheet.

1.   What will be done with most of the old cameras?   __will be sold_____

2.   What is about to be bought?   __new or color cameras_____

3.   Has information already been sent out about how to use the
new cameras?   ____no_____

4.   What is the limit on how long the color cameras may be kept?   ____three days_____

5.   What is being kept for use over longer periods of time?

_____a few black-and-white cameras_____

MASTERY REQUIREMENT: 4 correct responses

Indicate mastery on the student response sheet with a check.

IV. ORAL AND SILENT READING

    C. Listening

        1. Comprehends material
            read by another

Name _____

Date _____

Mastery _____

DIRECTIONS: Answer these questions about the information you just heard read.

1. What will be done with most of the old cameras?

_____

2. What is about to be bought?

_____

3. Has information already been sent out about how to use the new cameras?

_____

4. What is the limit on how long the color cameras may be kept?

_____

5. What is being kept for use over longer periods of time?

_____

IV. ORAL AND SILENT READING   C. Listening   2. **Can follow directions read aloud**

OBJECTIVE: The student will follow directions read aloud.

DIRECTIONS: Listen closely and do what you are instructed to do.

1. Near the center of your student response sheet, write your name, last name first.

2. Just below that, write your date of birth this way: first the day, then the month spelled out in full, then the last two numerals of the year.

3. At the bottom right corner of the sheet, write our room number, which is _____.

4. Just on the left edge of your paper, about halfway down from the top, draw a circle about the size of a dime, and fill it in completely.

MASTERY REQUIREMENT: All correct (Don't be overly concerned about neatness, as children are working on unlined paper.)

Indicate mastery on the student response sheet with a check.

IV. ORAL AND SILENT READING

    C. Listening

        2. Can follow directions
            read aloud

Name _____

Date _____

Mastery _____